BLACK BOOK OF

ROME

*The Timeless Guide to
the Eternal City*

VESNA NESKOW

ILLUSTRATED BY
KERREN BARBAS STECKLER

PETER PAUPER PRESS, INC.
WHITE PLAINS, NEW YORK

FOR MY SISTER ELIZABETH,
A GREAT TRAVEL COMPANION

Editor: Mara Conlon
Proofreader: JCommunications, LLC
Designed by Heather Zschock
Illustrations copyright © 2007 Kerren Barbas Steckler
Rome Transportation map © 2006 ATAC S.P.A.
Used with permission.
Neighborhood maps © 2010 David Lindroth Inc.

Copyright © 2010
Peter Pauper Press, Inc.
202 Mamaroneck Avenue
White Plains, NY 10601
All rights reserved
ISBN 978-1-59359-776-4
Printed in Hong Kong
7 6 5 4 3 2

The publisher has made every effort to ensure that the content of this book was current at time of publication. It's always best, however, to confirm information before making final travel plans, since telephone numbers, Web sites, prices, hours of operation, and other facts are always subject to change. The publisher cannot accept responsibility for any consequences arising from the use of this book. We value your feedback and suggestions. Please write to: Editors, Peter Pauper Press, Inc., 202 Mamaroneck Avenue, Suite 400, White Plains, New York 10601-5376.

Visit us at www.peterpauper.com

THE LITTLE
BLACK BOOK OF
ROME

CONTENTS

INTRODUCTION

Rome, the Eternal City. Its epithet says it all: history and modernity play equal parts in making Rome timeless, magical. More than 2,700 years of numerous civilizations coexist side by side or piled on top of each other. Founded in 753 BC, the Iron Age village became the most sophisticated city of Europe—first through a short Etruscan period, then

with the birth of the Republic and the powerful Roman Empire, which expanded its boundaries of influence throughout Europe and North Africa. But the Romans were neither the first nor the last—perhaps only the most spectacular—to teach us that power breeds corruption, greed, and decadence. Democracy gave way to dictatorship and eventually Rome declined as an empire, leaving the control of the city to a medieval clergy whose lust for power was hardly hidden. Luckily, the Middle Ages were followed by the Renaissance and the Baroque eras, and Rome flourished with great art and architecture for several centuries. In 1870, adjoining city-states were unified and Italy came into being with Rome as its capital.

Today, that rich history has made Rome a living museum. The best way by far to see Rome is to wander through its streets. Stumble across its splendors. Turn the corner and let yourself be awed by a sumptuous fountain, a Bernini sculpture, a Baroque obelisk, or an ancient arch. Or maybe a diminutive Madonna, sculpted into the corner of an ochre-colored building, seeming to watch over you as your feet take your heart on a tour of discovery. Splendor, drama, and romance are all built right into the city. It's voluptuous and it's erotic. Rome is glorious—and it's all on show.

Rome isn't just a museum, however. Its citizens wear their history with pride but live in the present. The city pulses with new technology, and the latest in art, architecture, fashion, and culinary wizardry bring modern pilgrims to the City of the Seven Hills. Ultra-modern architecture, such as the Auditorium-Parco della Musica, places Rome squarely among the leading cities shaping the vision and form of the 21st-century metropolis.

Yet Romans themselves accept change with a shrug of the shoulders. They like their city's reputation as *Caput Mundi*, but being *Head of the World* should not mean giving up their leisurely pace of life, taking pleasure in the daily rituals that give substance to the existence. When Fellini made *La Dolce Vita*, it wasn't by chance that he shot the film in Rome, where "the sweet life" is the only way to live. To this day, Romans still close shop at least an hour for lunch. They meet neighbors at local bars and greet acquaintances during the evening stroll along the Via del Corso. The piazza—the city square—is truly a meeting place: governments may fall, film stars may scandalize, globalization may transform old-fashioned businesses, but Romans continue to fill the piazza, interacting and expressing themselves as exuberantly and as warmly today as they did millennia ago. The fascination of Rome is as much in its people as in its places and objects.

This guidebook is meant to assist you in discovering that allure. All the splendors of Rome are too numerous to include in any one book; this one will introduce you to some of its highlights to help you embark on your exploration of this magical city. As you discover Rome, you will also discover yourself. It's a journey of love. After all, as any Roman will tell you with delight, *Roma* (the Italian for "Rome") is *Amor* spelled backwards. So let *Love* be your guide as you tuck this book into your pocket and set foot onto cobblestones that have been trod by Julius Caesar, Agrippina, Michelangelo,

Artemisia Gentileschi, Galileo, Pier Paolo Pasolini, and Renzo Piano. The brilliance and genius of the Eternal City will surely touch your spirit.

HOW TO USE THIS GUIDE

Each chapter is divided into clusters of neighborhoods. A fold-out map is included for each chapter with color-coded numbers corresponding to the places mentioned in the text. **Red** symbols indicate **Places to See** (landmarks and arts & entertainment). **Blue** symbols indicate **Places to Eat & Drink** (restaurants, cafés, bars, and nightlife). **Orange** symbols indicate **Where to Shop**. **Green** symbols indicate **Where to Stay**. Some shops and restaurants are closed in July and August, so check before going. Each place mentioned is followed by its address, local telephone number, Web site, and hours, if available.

Here are our keys for restaurant and hotel costs:

Restaurants
Cost of an appetizer and main course without drinks

(€)	Up to €25
(€€)	€25-€50
(€€€)	€50-€75
(€€€€)	€75 and up

Hotels
Cost per room per night

(€)	Up to €150
(€€)	€150-€250
(€€€)	€250-€400
(€€€€)	€400 and up

Abbreviations

B	bus line
M	metropolitana (subway) station
P.za	piazza (square)

ALL ABOUT MONEY

Money changing

The currency in Italy is euros (€). Most places accept credit cards. For cash withdrawals in Euros, ATMs *(bancomat)* offer good exchange rates. (Contact your bank before leaving home to determine if you need an international PIN for your cash card or credit cards.) Exchange rates for cash or travelers' checks are best in banks (usually open Monday-Friday, 8:30AM-4PM, closed for lunch), bad at the many independent exchange bureaux *(cambio)*, and worst at hotels and shops. You can also change money and get tourist information at **American Express** *(P.za di Spagna 38, Tel. 06-676.41; hours: M–F 9AM-5:30PM, Sa 9AM–12:30PM).*

Tipping

Tipping is a gray area, but don't look to Italians: foreigners should tip more than locals. If a service charge isn't included in your restaurant bill, a 10% tip is generally appropriate; if it's included, leave small change. At casual places, €1-5 is OK. For drinks at bar counters, leave small change. For taxis, round up the fare. Leave housekeeping and bellboys €1-2; the concierge, €2-3. Theatre ushers are tipped at least 50¢.

Euro-sense

Decimal points and commas are reversed from the U.S. system. So euros are separated from euro-cents *(centesimi)* by a comma, and hundreds are separated from thousands by a period (e.g., €2.425,50).

PUBLIC TRANSPORTATION

Getting to and from the Airport

Rome has two major airports: Leonardo da Vinci-Fiumicino *(colloquially, "Fiumicino," after the town where it is located, Tel. 06-65.951/06-6595.3640, www.adr.it)* and Ciampino *(Tel. 06-65.951/06-6595.9515, www.adr.it)*, which services mostly charter flights. Flights from the U.S. would go to Fiumicino. A taxi from Fiumicino to Rome costs at least €40. Book a taxi through Airport Connection Services *(06-338.32.21)*, P.I.T. inside the airport *(Tourist Information Point of Rome)*, or the airport taxi service *(06-6595.3794)*.

An **express train service** goes from Fiumicino to Rome's main train station, Stazione Termini, every 30 minutes from about 6AM to about 11PM. It takes 31 minutes and costs €11. The **regular train service** goes to Trastevere, Ostiense, Tuscolana, and Tiburtina stations; it takes 25-40 minutes and costs €5. Tickets can be purchased in the airport lobby or train stations. Before boarding you must stamp your ticket in the machines on the train station platform.

Terravision **coaches** *(06-6595.8646, www.terravision.it)* run between Fiumicino and Termini *(opposite Royal Santina Hotel, via Marsala 22; hours: M–Su 8AM–8PM)* every two hours during the day. They take 70 minutes and cost €9 one way, €15 round trip. **Night buses** run every hour or so between Fiumicino-Termini-Tiburtina and cost €5 one way. The train stations are a bit unsafe at night (and a known haven for pickpockets), so it's best to take a taxi there and back.

Metro & Bus Tickets

The city transport system *(run by ATAC, www.atac. roma.it)* consists of buses, trams, and metro (subway). There are only two metro lines, so buses are usually the better bet. You will find a public transportation map in the back of this book. We've introduced each section with a listing of several different bus routes you can use to get to the neighborhood (and metro information, if applicable). Within the center of the city, walking is your best means of transport.

You can buy tickets at newspaper kiosks, tobacconist shops *(tabacchi)*, or metro stations. You must validate your ticket at the beginning of your trip by punching it in one of the machines on the bus or at the metro station. A BIT ticket, for unlimited bus trips and one metro trip, is valid for 75 minutes and costs €1. A one-day BIG ticket gets you anywhere in Rome for €4. The three-day BTI pass, €11, covers city buses, metro, and trains to Ostia (second class). The weekly CIS pass costs €16.

Taxis

Taxis are best requested by phone *(06-35.70; 06-49.94; 06-66.45; 06-88.22)*. Expect extra charges for luggage, night fares, and rides outside the city. Round up your fare to include a small tip.

Boat Tours

Rides down the Tiber come without commentary for
(€1), with guides (€12), or as dinner tours (€54). Tickets
can be purchased from Battelli di Roma *(06-9774.5498,
www.battellidiroma.it)* at the jetty or online.

Bike/Scooter/Moped Rentals

It might be daunting to join Roman drivers on the
streets, but bikes, scooters, and mopeds are convenient
for getting around parks and more distant areas. Here
are some places that rent such vehicles, by district:

TRIDENTE/VILLA BORGHESE: Biciroma *(bikes, mopeds)*,
P.za del Popolo; P.za di Spagna; Pincio Gardens

VIA VENETO/VILLA BORGHESE: I Bike Rome *(bikes, scooters, mopeds)*, Villa Borghese underground parking, Via
Veneto, 06-322.52.40

VIA VENETO: Scooters for Rent *(bikes, mopeds)*, Via della
Purificazione 84, 06-488.54.85, *www.travel.it/roma/
scooters*

CAMPO DEI FIORI/GHETTO: Collalti *(bikes)*, Via del

Pellegrino 82, 06-68.80.10.84;
RomaRent *(bikes, scooters,
mopeds, bike tours)*, Vicolo dei
Bovari 7A, 06-689.65.55, *web.
tiscali.it/romarent*

ESQUILINO/MONTI: Happy Rent/
Due Ruote Rent *(scooters, mopeds)*,

Via Farini 3, 06-481.81.85; Treno e Scooter Rent *(bikes, scooters, mopeds)*, Termini Station, 06-488.27.97; Scoot-a-Long *(scooters, mopeds)*, Via Cavour 302, 06-678.02.06

MAKING PHONE CALLS

The area code for Rome is 06. When dialing within Italy or Rome, dial the number as it appears, including the 06 area code for Rome. Italian 800 area codes are toll-free. Note: phone numbers in Rome consist of the area code plus 5, 6, 7, or 8 digits. To make an international call from Rome, dial 00 plus country code (1 for U.S.), area code, and number. When calling Rome direct from the U.S., dial 011-39, then the full number.

MEALS

In Italy, pasta is a course, not a meal. The main courses are: *antipasto* (appetizer), *primo* (small pasta portion), and *secondo* (entrée). It's usual in Italy to eat a *primo* and *secondo*. And don't forget the *dolci* (desserts)!

SHOPPING

Hours: Shop hours are generally 9AM–1PM and 3:30PM–7:30PM (4PM–8PM in summer). Some shops stay open from 10AM–7:30PM. Many shops close during the lunch hours, from 2PM–4PM or 1PM–3:30PM. *Chiuso per Ferie* means the shop is closed for vacation, mostly in August, sometimes July. Most shops are closed on Sundays and in the summer on Saturday afternoons (Monday mornings in winter).

Sales: Sales (*saldi*) are held twice a year, mid-January through February, and mid-July through mid-September. Otherwise, good deals are marked in stores as "*promozioni.*"

Tax Refunds: In stores with a "Europe Tax Free" or "Global Refund" sticker, non-EU citizens can get a refund for part of the sales tax if you spend a minimum of €155 in that store on one day. You must show your passport and you'll be given a form in the store. When leaving Italy, go to the customs office at the airport and have your form stamped (Global Refund Office, Fiumicino Airport, Terminals B and C). You'll have to show your passport and store receipt. You may have to show your purchases, so it's best to do this before check-in, or else keep your purchases in your carry-on. Once home, return one copy of the form in the envelope provided and keep the other copy for yourself. You must do this within 90 days of the purchase.

If traveling to other EU countries, get your forms stamped in the airport customs office of the last EU country you leave. It takes about three months to get the refund. You might be able to get your refund at a Global Refund office in Rome by the Spanish Steps at P.za Trinità dei Monti 17/A.

Department Stores: La Rinascente and Coin are Italy's largest chain department stores, with outlets throughout Rome. Upim is a chain discount store.

SAY IT IN ITALIAN

A phrase book is always good to have on hand, but you might want to learn some basic words and phrases.

Parla inglese? *(PAR-lah een-GLAY-zeh)* Do you speak English?

Buon giorno *(boo-ohn GEOR-no)* Good morning (before lunch)

Buona sera *(boo-ohna SEHR-ah)* Good afternoon/evening (after lunch)

Buona notte *(boo-ohna NOH-tay)* Good night

Arrivederci *(ah-ree-veh-DEHR-chee)* Good-bye

Ciao *(CHOW)* Hi/'Bye

Per favore *(pair fah-VOH-reh)* Please

Vorrei *(voh-RAY)* I'd like

Grazie *(GRAH-tsee-yay)* Thank you

Prego *(PREY-go)* You're welcome

Permesso *(pair-MESS-oh)* Excuse me (to move past someone in a crowd)

Mi scusi *(me SCOO-zee)* Excuse me (to get attention; sorry)

Mi dispiace *(me dees-pee-YA-cheh)* I'm sorry

Va bene *(vah BEH-neh)* OK/That's OK

Aspetta *(ahss-PET-ah)* Wait

Andiamo *(ahn-dee-YA-moh)* Let's go

Sì *(SEE)* Yes

No *(NOH)* No

Dov'è… *(doh-VEH)* Where is…

la metropolitana *(la metro-polee-TAH-na)* subway

metro *(met-ROH)* subway (short version)

un biglietto *(oon bee-LEEYE-toh)* a ticket

17

la strada *(la STRAH-da)* the street

via *(VEE-yah)* street (name)

l'albergo *(l'ahl-BEAR-goh)* hotel

il negozio *(il neh-GOH-tsee-oh)* store

il ristorante *(il ree-stoh-RAHN-teh)* restaurant

il palazzo *(il pah-LAH-tsoh)* apartment building; palace; mansion

la piazza *(la pee-AH-tsah)* square (town square)

Dove sono i gabinetti? *(DOH-veh SOH-noh ee gab-ee-NET-ee)* Where is the bathroom?

Quanto costa? *(KWAN-toh COST-ah)* How much does it cost?

Signora *(see-NYO-rah)* Ma'am, Mrs.

Signorina *(see-nyo-REE-nah)* Miss

Signor/Signore *(see-NYO-reh)* Sir, Mr.

cameriere *(kahm-air-ee-AIR-eh)* waiter

cameriera *(kahm-ahr-ee-AIR-ah)* waitress

chi *(KEE)* who

cosa *(KOH-ZA)* what

Cos'è? *(koz-EH)* What is it?

dove *(DOH-veh)* where

come *(KOH-meh)* how

quanti *(KWAHN-tee)* many, how many

quanto *(KWAHN-toh)* much, how much

quando *(KWAHN-doh)* when

colazione *(koh-lah-tsee-OH-neh)* breakfast

pranzo *(PRAHN-tsoh)* lunch

cena *(CHEH-na)* dinner

ETIQUETTE TIPS

When entering a shop always say, "Buon giorno" ("Good morning"—before lunch) or "Buona sera" ("Good afternoon"—after lunch). Before handling merchandise, ask, "Posso?" (May I?).

It's more polite to add "Signore" or "Signora" when greeting someone—though just saying "Buon giorno" or "Buona sera" without the title is not rude.

To get the attention of a waiter, call out "Senta!" (literally, "Listen!") or "Scusi!" ("Excuse me").

ON THE TOWN: PLAYS, CONCERTS, EVENTS, EXHIBITS

BOOKING TICKETS: Tickets for theatre and classical concerts are usually purchased at the theatre. Tickets for rock, jazz, and classical concerts as well as certain sports events can also be obtained at the **Ricordi** music store's "Box Office" *(Via del Corso 506, 06-361.23.70)* and at **Orbis** *(P.za del Esquilino 37, 06-482.74.03)*.

LISTINGS: Listings magazines for arts, entertainment, and other events include **L'Evento** (available at APT—*see page 21*), the weekly magazine **Roma c'è** (with an English "Week in Rome" section), and **Trovaroma**, a supplement to the Thursday edition of the newspaper *La Repubblica*.

FREE CONCERTS: Tourist info booths offer pamphlets listing free concerts *(see page 21)*. Churches and foreign institutes give free concerts. The latter include the Belgian Academy *(via Omero 8, 06-320.18.89)*, the Austrian Cultural Institute *(viale Bruno Buozzi 113, 06-360.83.71)*, the Japanese Cultural Institute *(via Gramsci 74, 06-322.47.94)*, and the Hungarian Academy *(via Giulia 1, 06-688.96.71)*. The Music Festival sponsors all sorts of free concerts around the city every June 21st.

PARCO DELLA MUSICA *(Viale Pietro de Coubertin 30, 06-80.24.12.81, www.auditorium.com, B: 53, 910)*, less than two miles north of Piazza del Popolo, is Rome's premier auditorium for classical music.

MACRO *(Via Reggio Emilia 54, 06-67.10.70.400, www.macro.roma.museum, B: 36, 60, 84, 90)*, the Museum for Contemporary Art of Rome, is an exciting center featuring Italian art since the 1960s.

MAXXI *(Via Guido Reni 2f, 06-321.01.81, www.maxxi. darc.beniculturali.it, B: 19, 53, 217, 225, 910)*, the National Museum of 21st-Century Art, is an exhibition and performance space. At the time of this publication it was still in the construction phase; however, temporary exhibits are being held in a nearby hangar.

FORO ITALICO—Sports Arenas *(P.za L. de Bosis/via del Foro Italico, B: 32, 224, 280)* is where Rome's major-league soccer teams, AS Roma *(www.asroma.it)* and SS Lazio *(www.sslazio.it)*, compete. The Italian Open is held at the nearby tennis courts *(see Seasonal Events, page 23)*.

TOURIST INFORMATION

Web sites: Several sites give helpful general information and updates on exhibitions, events, festivals, bars, nightclubs, etc. These include:

www.italiantourism.com
www.comune.roma.it/cultura
www.romaturismo.it
www.capitolium.org
www.romainweb.com (Italian only)

Italian Tourist Offices in US:
NY: 212-245-5618/4822
LA: 310-820-1898/0098

Tourist Offices in Rome:
The **APT** (Azienda di Promozione Turistica) gives information, free brochures, and free city maps.

APT in Rome: Via Parigi 5, Esquilino, 06-48.89.91; hours: M-Sa 9AM-7PM
APT at Fiumicino Airport: Terminal B, 06 65.95.60.74/ 06-65.95.94.23; hours: daily 8:15AM–7:30PM

Information kiosks around the city:
Termini Station: Platform 2 (06-48.90.63.00)
Termini Station: Piazza dei Cinquecento (06-47.82.51.94)
Fori Imperiali: Piazza Tempio della Pace (06-69.92.43.07)
Piazza di Spagna: Largo Goldoni (06-68.13.60.61)

Piazza Navona: Piazza Cinque Lune (06-68.80.92.40)
Via Nazionale: Palazzo delle Esposizioni (06-47.82.45.25)
Trastevere: Piazza Sonnino (06-58.33.34.57)
San Giovanni: Piazza San Giovanni in Laterano (06-77.20.35.35)
Castel Sant'Angelo: Piazza Pia (06-68.80.97.07)

SEASONAL EVENTS

Romans will do anything for a party, and just about any saint's day is reason enough to hold a festival. The weather sometimes inspires all-night bashes. Spring and autumn are the best seasons in Rome. Winter tends to be rainy, while summer is very hot. Most Romans leave the city in August and often in July as well.

Spring:

Rome Marathon (3rd or 4th Sunday in March)—on city streets, begins and ends on via dei Fori Imperiali *(Maratona di Roma, 06-406.50.64, www.maratonadi roma.it)*.

Easter (March/April)—Holy Week is marked by services throughout Rome and open-air masses at St. Peter's Square; the pope leads the Stations of the Cross and mass on Good Friday *(Colosseum, late evening)* and addresses the people gathered in St. Peter's Square on Easter Sunday *(P.za San Pietro, Vatican)*.

Rome's Birthday—April 21 (or preceding Sunday)—Fireworks at Piazza del Campidoglio mark the founding of Rome in 753 BC.

Via Margutta Art Fair (4–5 days, April–May, also October–November) —Art galleries on a charming street once full of artists' studios open their doors *(Via Margutta, 06-812.33.40, www. centopittoriviamargutta.it).*

Settimana della Cultura—Culture Week (April/May)—Many museums, archaeological sites, and cultural centers offer free admission; some normally restricted archives open their doors to the public; and special artistic and cultural events take place *(800-991.199, www.beniculturali.it).*

International Horse Show (late April–early May)—The world's elite equestrians gather for this prestigious show-jumping event. *(P.za di Siena, Villa Borghese, 06-3685.8470/06-638.38.18, www.piazzadisiena.com, www.fise.it).*

May Day—Primo Maggio (May 1)—A free rock concert sponsored by labor unions; it marks International Workers' Day *(P.za di San Giovanni in Laterano).*

Italian Open Tennis Tournament (2 weeks, early May)—An international tennis event *(Foro Italico, viale dei Gladiatori 31, northern outskirts, toll-free 800-622.662, www.federtennis.it).*

Summer:

Festival Internazionale delle Letterature (May–June)—In an ancient setting, renowned writers from around the world read from their work *(Basilica di Massenzio, enter at Clivo di Venere Felice in via dei Fori Imperiali, 06-06.08, www.letterature.festivalroma.org; hours: daily 9AM–10:30PM)*.

Estate Romana (Roman Summer) (June–September)—A popular festival featuring plays, dance, concerts, opera, and films, all in outdoor venues, many free *(check local press listings, www.estateromana.it)*.

Political Party Festivals (June–September)—Free open-air events, street fairs, concerts, and performances are organized by political parties. These are family-oriented events and everyone goes, regardless of political affiliation; the biggest is Festa dell'Unità, the Communists' bash *(various venues, check listings)*.

Isola del Cinema (June–August)—This indie film festival held in an open-air cinema on Tiber Island spotlights emerging directors. Bars and restaurants help make it more than a night at the movies *(Isola Tiberina, www.isoladelcinema.com)*.

Alta Roma Fashion Week (July; January)—Designers present their new lines in historical venues; though by invitation only, you can squeeze in the back or find an elevated spot from which to peek at the drama of high fashion *(check local listings)*.

Festa dei Noantri (last 2 weeks of July)—Trastevere celebrates its working-class origins with an open-air carnival, replete with music, performances, street fairs, and fireworks *(P.za Santa Maria in Trastevere, P.za Mastai)*.

Ferragosto (Feast of the Assumption) (August 15)—Those who've stayed in the city take a long weekend for this holy day, and Rome practically closes down—a good time to go to the beach.

Autumn:

Enzimi (September, 2 weeks)—The cutting edge in creative talent debuts at this free festival of the arts. Theatre, dance, and music events *(various venues)* are especially interesting.

La Notte Bianca (September/October, a Saturday)—For one day, museums, archaeological sites, artists' studios, restaurants, shops, and bars are open all night; street parties abound *(various venues, 06-06.06, www.lanotte bianca.it)*.

RomaEuropa Festival (September–November)—This very cool performing arts festival brings together avant-garde and classical dance, theatre, and music *(various venues, 06-422.961, www.romaeuropa.net)*.

Via Margutta Art Fair (4–5 days, October–November) *(see page 23, Spring)*.

Antiques Fair (October/November, 2 weeks; also April/May, some years)—Antique collectors flock here each year *(Via dei Coronari, 06-686.53.47, www.assviadeicoronari.it)*.

Winter:

Christmas (December 24–25)—The pope celebrates midnight mass on Christmas Eve *(St. Peter's Basilica, Vatican; for tickets, fax the Prefect of the Pontifical Household, 06-69.88.58.63, www.vatican.va)* and blesses the crowds in St. Peter's Square on Christmas Day *(noon, Vatican).*

New Year's (December 31–January 1)—Fireworks and a free concert in Piazza del Popolo on New Year's Eve are brilliant and fairly raucous. Check out the crazy river divers, who plunge into the Tiber from the Cavour Bridge on New Year's Day.

Alta Roma Fashion Week (January) *(see page 24, Summer).*

ROME'S TOP PICKS

TOP PICK!

Rome offers an abundance of one-of-a-kind attractions and experiences for visitors. Here are 13 of the top picks not to be missed!

★ **Piazza Navona** *(see page 32)*
★ **National Museum of Rome—Palazzo Altemps** *(see page 34)*
★ **Pantheon** *(see page 40)*
★ **Spanish Steps** *(see page 59)*
★ **Villa Borghese/Galleria Borghese** *(see page 71)*
★ **Trevi Fountain** *(see page 78)*
★ **Santa Maria Maggiore** *(see page 85)*
★ **San Pietro in Vincoli** *(see page 85)*
★ **Capitoline Museums** *(see page 123)*
★ **Colosseum/Roman Forum** *(see pages 126-134)*
★ **St. Peter's Basilica** *(see pages 186-188)*
★ **Raphael Rooms/Sistine Chapel** *(see page 190)*
★ **Baths of Caracalla** *(see page 112)*

chapter 1

PIAZZA NAVONA

PANTHEON

CAMPO DEI FIORI/GHETTO

PIAZZA NAVONA
PANTHEON
CAMPO DEI FIORI/GHETTO

Places to See:

1. PIAZZA NAVONA ★
2. Fountain of the Four Rivers
3. Sant'Agnese in Agone
4. Santa Maria della Pace
5. Chiesa Nuova
6. Pasquino
7. Palazzo Madama
8. San Luigi dei Francesi
9. Museum of Rome
10. NATIONAL MUSEUM OF ROME—PALAZZO ALTEMPS ★
11. Teatro Valle
32. PANTHEON ★
33. Santa Maria sopra Minerva
34. Gesù
35. Temple of Hadrian
36. Column of Marcus Aurelius
37. Galleria Alberto Sordi
38. Palazzo Doria Pamphili
54. Campo dei Fiori
55. Palazzo Farnese
56. Palazzo Spada
57. Galleria Spada
58. Sant'Andrea della Valle
59. Largo Argentina Sacred Precincts
60. Crypta Balbi
61. Fountain of the Tortoises
62. Via Giulia
63. Portico d'Ottavia
64. Theatre of Marcellus
65. Synagogue
66. Museum of Jewish Culture
67. Isola Tiberina
68. Ponte Rotto
69. Piccola Farnesina
70. Teatro Argentina

Places to Eat & Drink:

12. Hostaria dell'Orso
13. Santa Lucia
14. Antica Biblioteca
15. Da Baffetto
16. Raphaël
17. Bloom
18. Via della Pace
19. Bar della Pace
20. La Maison
21. Casa Bleve
39. Maccheroni
40. Osteria dell'Ingegno
41. Caffè Sant'Eustachio
42. Tazza d'Oro
43. Riccioli Café

★ *Top Picks*

PIAZZA NAVONA

B: 46, 62, 64, 70, 81, 87, 116, 492, 628

• SNAPSHOT •

The *centro storico*—"historical center"—of Rome covers an area stretching as far east as the Colosseum, and as far west as the Castel Sant' Angelo, across the Tiber River. Included in the *centro storico* is the Piazza Navona area nestled within the bend of the Tiber. The actual Piazza Navona, built in the oblong shape of an ancient racetrack, was constructed on the ruins of a stadium built by Emperor Domitian.

Today, the arena is decidedly Baroque, with fountains and a church created by two of that period's greatest artists, Bernini and Borromini. In some ways the lifestyle of the Piazza Navona area, too, is Baroque: booths of kitschy tourist souvenirs co-exist with posh restaurants and hip bars. By day it's all business; after dark it becomes a nocturnal Cinderella, attracting princes and chimney sweeps with its charm.

Piazza Navona itself and the winding streets of the *centro storico* are magnificent. Wander the streets. You can't get lost—the area is small enough to maneuver easily with a map. You'll feel like an explorer or relic hunter. Narrow byways, spectacular fountains, ancient churches, boisterous denizens—the area surrounding Piazza Navona can leave you breathless.

PLACES TO SEE
Landmarks:

In the first century, athletic games were held in a large stadium in what is today's ★**PIAZZA NAVONA (1)**. The piazza is a marvel of Baroque art and architecture. People flock there to sit and enjoy the sights and sounds of Rome's most famous piazza. Three incredible fountains grace the long esplanade. The **Fountain of the Four Rivers (2)**, designed by the master sculptor Bernini, depicts rivers that represent four continents: the Nile (Africa), Ganges (Asia), Danube (Europe), and Plata (South America). The other two fountains, the *Fountain of the Moor* and *Neptune's Fountain*, are also fabulous. Along the western flank of Piazza Navona is the **Sant'Agnese in Agone (3)** *(06-68.19.21.34, www.sant agneseinagone.org; hours: Tu–Su 9:30AM–12:30PM, 3:30PM–7PM, holidays 10AM–1PM, 4PM–7PM)* church, notable not only because it was made by Bernini's rival Borromini, but also because of the gutsy 13-year-old martyr it's named after. Agnes, a 4th-century girl, refused to renounce Christianity or marry the Roman suitors who fell for her. Some say she was stripped and strung out on the site, but her hair grew miraculously and covered her nude body. She was ultimately beheaded. Ruins of Emperor Domitian's stadium can be seen below the church.

Like much of Rome, the area abounds with churches and sculptured buildings. Walking through the quarter will bring you face to face with statues, columns, capitols, friezes, portals—all the drama and flamboyance of Renaissance and Baroque Rome. Raphael's famous *Sybils* fresco is the high point of **Santa Maria della Pace (4)** *(Vicolo del Arco della Pace 5, 06-686.11.56)*. And its lovely Bramante cloister has a bookshop and bar.

In 1575 Filippo Neri built **Chiesa Nuova (5)** *(P.za della Chiesa Nuova, 06-687.52.89, www.vallicella.org; hours: Winter 7:30AM–12PM, 4:30PM–7:15PM, Summer 7:30AM–12PM, 4:30PM–7:30PM)*, teaching humility to the Roman noblemen among his followers by making them do the work. Above and on either side of the altar are three Rubens paintings. For more Roman wit, make a beeline for **Pasquino (6)** *(P.za di Pasquino)*, the "talking" statue. Named after a 15th-century cobbler who wasn't fond of how the papacy curbed freedom of speech, Pasquino wrote out his gripes satirizing the ruling classes, then stuck them on the statue. Soon it became the rage to speak your mind through statues.

The spectacularly ornate **Palazzo Madama (7)** *(Corso del Rinascimento, 06-6706.3430, www.senato.it/english)*, once a Medici family palace, houses the Senate, the upper house of the Italian parliament. Three Caravaggios hang in **San Luigi dei Francesi (8)** *(P.za di*

WHERE TO SHOP

It's a delight to stroll down **Via dei Coronari (22)** and browse the shops for antiques and Art Nouveau pieces. **Via del Governo Vecchio (23)**, once part of the itinerary of papal processions (Via Papalis) between the Lateran and the Vatican in the 15th century, now packs fashionable stores among the 15th- and 16th-century houses. For example, **Josephine de Huertas & Co. (24)** *(Via del Governo Vecchio 68, 06-687.65.86, www.josephinede huertas.com)* offers an eclectic mix of clothes with sensual fabrics, textures, and lines. At **Jade & More (25)** *(Via del Governo Vecchio 36, 06-683.39.36)* elegant designs with retro influences are created and crafted by Cristina Jadeluca. Look for vintage clothes at **Vestiti Usati Cinzia (26)** *(Via del Governo Vecchio 45, 06-683.29.45).*

WHERE TO STAY

The rooms at friendly Hotel Rinascimento (83) (€) *(Via del Pellegrino 122, 06-687.48.13, www.hotelrinascimento.com)* are small, but a good deal. You'll love the views from the rooftop terrace of the comfortable Hotel Campo de' Fiori (84) (€-€€) *(Via del Biscione 6, 06-68.80.68.65, www.hotelcampodefiori.com)*, but not all rooms have private baths. Tucked into a street of artisans' workshops, Relais Banchi Vecchi (85) (€-€€) *(Via dei Banchi Vecchi 115, 06-321.17.83, www.banchivecchi115.com)* is exceptionally charming, with authentic historical touches. It reflects the style of its director, former concert pianist Milena Stojkovic, and its simply-furnished rooms are complemented by large marble and tile bathrooms. Staying at Hotel Cardinal (86) (€€) *(Via Giulia 62, 06-68.80.27.19, from U.S. 1-800-523-8561)* is almost like extending your museum visits; it was designed by Donato Bramante (who also designed St. Peter's Basilica). The granite of the bar was taken from the Roman Forum. On the remains of the Theater of Pompey, where Caesar was assassinated in 44 BC, Hotel Teatro di Pompeo (87) (€-€€) *(Largo del Pallaro 8, 06-687.28.12/06-68.30.01.70, web.tiscali.it/hotel_teatrodipompeo)* offers small but pleasing rooms with unpretentious décor.

chapter 2

TRIDENTE/PIAZZA
DI SPAGNA
VIA VENETO
VILLA BORGHESE

TRIDENTE/PIAZZA DI SPAGNA
VIA VENETO
VILLA BORGHESE

Places to See:

1. Porta del Popolo
2. Piazza del Popolo
3. Santa Maria del Popolo
4. Ara Pacis
5. Mausoleum of Augustus
9. SPANISH STEPS ★
10. Boat Fountain
11. Pincio Gardens
12. Keats-Shelley Memorial House
13. Casa-Museo Giorgio De Chirico
33. Piazza di Spagna
29. Santa Maria della Vittoria
30. Piazza Barberini
31. Via Veneto
32. Santa Maria della Concezione
33. Palazzo Barberini
48. Temple of Diana
49. Temple of Aesculapius
50. Bioparco
51. GALLERIA BORGHESE ★
52. National Gallery of Modern Art
53. Villa Giulia

Places to Eat & Drink:

14. Dal Bolognese
15. Gina
16. Reef
17. Bar Canova
18. Caffè Greco
19. Gregory's
34. La Terrazza dell'Eden
35. Papà Baccus
37. Moma
38. Jasmine
40. Sala degli Angeli, Café de Paris
41. Doney
42. San Marco
54. Baby
55. Piazza di Siena Art Caffè

Where to Shop:

6. Via dei Condotti
7. Via Borgognona
8. Via Frattina
20. Battistoni
21. Via Bocca di Leone
22. Sermoneta
23. Il Discount dell'Alta Moda
24. Piazza di San Lorenzo in Lucina

★ *Top Picks*

All roads lead to Rome.

—Proverb

B: 116, 117, 119
M: A to Spagna

• SNAPSHOT •

The Tridente, an area extending southward from the Piazza del Popolo and including the Piazza di Spagna on the eastern border, gets its name from the three boulevards forking downward from Piazza del Popolo. The streets Via del Babuino, Via del Corso, and Via di Ripetta form a trident encompassing Rome's most posh area. Along with Via Veneto, the Tridente celebrates the glitz and glamour of the "jet set" memorialized in Federico Fellini's 1960 classic film *La Dolce Vita*. Aesthetes and artists have flocked to this quarter, along with film directors, actors, and international designers. For decades, it was a magnet for international literati, such as Keats, Shelley, and Byron.

Today, the Tridente is the most luxurious area of Rome, a mecca for high-style shoppers that is distinguished by its international ambience. Many of the city's most dignified hotels and distinctive restaurants are located in this quarter. Don't miss the Spanish Steps, rising above the Piazza di Spagna. From there, the gloriously breathtaking vista reminds you why Rome is the Eternal City.

PLACES TO SEE
Landmarks:

In the 3rd century the **Aurelian Wall** was constructed to protect the city from invaders, with entrance and exit portals at various points. The 16th-century **Porta del Popolo (1)** gateway was built by Pope Pius IV (Medici) on the site of the ancient *Porta Flaminia* as an impressive first view of Rome for VIP visitors entering from the north. Just inside the Porta del Popolo is the grandiose square **Piazza del Popolo (2)**. For centuries it was the papacy's preferred execution grounds. The square, one of Rome's largest, is lavish in architecture and artistry. Twin churches on the southern end of the enormous oval are remarkable in their neoclassical beauty. In the center, an ancient Egyptian obelisk is flanked by fountains with enormous marble lions spouting water from their mouths.

The church **Santa Maria del Popolo (3)** *(P.za del Popolo 12, 06-361.08.36; hours: daily 7AM–12PM, 4PM–7PM)* is one of Rome's gems of early Renaissance art, built in 1472 by Pope Sixtus IV della Rovere. It was said that Emperor Nero was secretly buried on the site; folk legend says that demons haunted the area, torturing Nero for his crimes, until the first church was built there in 1099. South of Piazza del Popolo, the **Ara Pacis (4)** *(Via di Ripetta/Lungotevere in Augusta, 06-67.10.67.56/06-36.00.43.99, www.arapacis.it; hours: Tu–Su 9AM–7PM)*, "Altar of Peace," is a monument and museum commemorating Emperor Augustus's conquest of Gaul and Spain and the ensuing peace. The area south of the monument was once the site of the **Mausoleum of Augustus (5)** *(P.za Augusto Imperatore; not open to the public)*, where the emperor's ashes were buried.

If ancient memorials aren't your cup of tea, you can join the thousands who gladly pay homage—and empty their wallets—to modern emperors of fashion and design in the well-planned streets between **Via del Corso** and **Via del Babuino**. Via dei Condotti (6), "Street of the Conduits," named after the ducts that brought water to the Baths of Agrippa near the Pantheon, is the most famous of these, closely followed by Via Borgognona (7) and Via Frattina (8).

One of the most popular spots in Rome is the ★**SPANISH STEPS (9)** *(Piazza di Spagna)*, named for the Spanish Embassy to the Vatican, housed near the base of the stairs. Built in grand Gallic style by a French financier between 1723 and 1726, they form an elegant staircase rising up the slope from **Piazza di Spagna (33)** to

the church of **Trinità dei Monti** *(P.za Trinità dei Monti 3, 06-679.41.79)* on Pincio Hill. In spring and summer, urns of azaleas are displayed on the steps, and fashion shows are held there. The area has been beloved of writers, artists, and musicians since the 18th century, most notable of which were Keats, Shelley, and De Chirico. At the foot of the Spanish Steps is the delightfully quirky **Boat Fountain (10)** *(P.za di Spagna)*, representing a leaky old boat that was said to have been stranded there when the Tiber overflowed.

From the top of the Steps, follow Viale della Trinità dei Monti to the **Pincio Gardens (11)** *(Pincio Hill)* for a fabulous view of Rome. Rock formations, magnificent tree-lined walks, and lovely benches make the elegant gardens, designed by the 19th-century's star architect Giuseppe Valadier, a favorite place for afternoon strolls or picnics.

Arts & Entertainment:

On Piazza di Spagna are two museum houses dedicated to artists who lived and worked there. The **Keats-Shelley Memorial House (12)** *(Piazza di Spagna 26, 06-678.42.35, www.keats-shelley-house.org; hours: M–F 10AM–1PM, 2PM–6PM, Sa 11AM–2PM, 3PM–6PM)*, the dusty pink building at the bottom of the Spanish Steps, contains all sorts of memorabilia related to the two English poets. Keats died there in 1821 at the age of 25, succumbing to tuberculosis and depression over bad reviews of his poetry. Both Keats and Shelley are buried

in Rome's Protestant Cemetery *(see page 152)*. More than 100 years later, another great artist died nearby, and his work space is now a museum: **Casa-Museo Giorgio De Chirico (13)** *(P.za di*

Spagna 31, 06-679.65.46; hours: by appt Tu–Sa 10AM–1PM, closed Aug) displays the palettes, brushes, and paints the Surrealist painter was working with just before his death, as well as other favorite objects and books.

PLACES TO EAT & DRINK
Where to Eat:
A classic of excellent traditional food, **Dal Bolognese (14)** (€€-€€€€) *(P.za del Popolo 1-2, 06-361.14.26; hours: Tu–Su 1PM–3PM, 8:15PM–12AM)* claims that "all Rome" comes by at some time or another. The view of the piazza and Pincio Hill, opposite, is great too. Hike up Pincio or to Villa Borghese with a picnic basket from **Gina (15)** (€) *(Via San Sebastianello 7/A, 06-678.02.51, www.ginaroma.com; hours: M–Sa 11AM–12AM, Su 11AM–8PM)* or sit inside the cool white rooms and feel summery all year round. **Reef (16)** (€€€) *(P.za Augusto Imperatore 42-48, 06-68.30.14.30; hours: M–Sa 1PM–3:30PM, 8PM–12AM)* is a Roman hot spot: the nautical décor, down to a glass floor through which you can see sand and water underneath, is matched by great fish and seafood.

Bars & Nightlife:
Piazza del Popolo was one of the spots where, up until the early 1990s, you could spot Italian movie stars and notables all the time. The back room at **Bar Canova (17)** *(P.za del Popolo 16-17,*

06-361.22.31; hours: daily 8AM–12/1AM) has been dedicated to Fellini, who lived nearby in Via Margutta 110 and regularly popped in for breakfast or an espresso.

The historic **Caffè Greco (18)** *(Via dei Condotti 86, 06-679.17.00; hours: M, Su 10:30AM–7PM, Tu–Sa 9AM–7:30PM)* was made famous by the artists and intellectuals who congregated there: Goethe, Byron, Keats, Liszt, Wagner, Bizet, Schopenhauer; then there were those, like Casanova and mad Bavarian King Ludwig, who also added color and notoriety to the place. **Gregory's (19)** *(Via Gregoriana 54A, 06-679.63.86, www.gregorysjazz.com; hours: Tu–Su 7PM–2AM)* is a cozy venue for good jazz and blues.

WHERE TO SHOP

High fashion is the name of the game in the Tridente. Haute couture pops from the windows of Renaissance palazzi in **Via dei Condotti (6)**, the street famous for designer shops, where you'll find Prada, Gucci, Ferragamo, Armani, and the most Roman of designers, Valentino. The gorgeous courtyard of **Battistoni (20)** *(Via dei Condotti 60-61a, 06-697.61.11)* prepares you for the

refinement inside. It's the epitome of the elegant Italian shop for classic, distinguished custom-made men's tailoring (although they also tailor for women).

In the next street over, **Via Borgognona (7)**, the showrooms include Fendi, Moschino, Zegna, and Versace (men).

For designers like Mariella Burani and Versace (women), it's **Via Bocca di Leone (21)**. Extraordinary handstitched gloves are the exemplary item at **Sermoneta (22)** *(P.za di Spagna 61, 06-679.19.60, www.sermonetagloves.com)*—not just cashmere, wool, and kid, but ostrich, boar, and crocodile, in sixty colors and six sizes.

If all the high-fashion boutiques leave you yearning for designer togs but your wallet keeps resisting, fear not: **Il Discount dell'Alta Moda (23)** *(Via di Gesù e Maria 14-16a, 06-361.37.96)* offers last season's designer clothes (men's and women's) at up to 80% discount. For a sense of old-fashioned Roman life, head to **Piazza di San Lorenzo in Lucina (24)**: the shops are classic, and the street life is delightfully relaxed.

WHERE TO STAY

Originally designed by Giuseppe Valadier (the 19th-century architect who laid out the **Pincio Gardens (11)** *(see page 60)*, as a residence for the Russian czar, **Hotel de Russie (25)** (€€€€) *(Via del Babuino 9, 06-32.88.81, www.hotelderussie.it)* is among Europe's top luxury hotels—and very expensive. Elegant in a modern reincarnation of its classical past, it has attracted famous artists, such as Picasso and Stravinsky.

Simplicity as luxury defines the four rooms of the **Palazzetto at the International Wine Academy (26)** (€€-€€€)

(Vicolo del Bottino 8, 06-699.08.78, www.wine academyroma.com) just off Piazza di Spagna. The roof terrace has wonderful views and hosts lovely wine tastings. Reasonable for the area, **Hotel Scalinata di Spagna (27) (€€)** *(P.za Trinità dei Monti 17, 06-69.94.08.96, www.hotelscalinata.com)* immerses you in a sense of luxury with its beautiful woodwork, exquisite gold-framed mirrors, and decidedly pampering chaise longues.

The exclusive **Hotel Hassler (28) (€€€€)** *(Piazza Trinità dei Monti 6, 06-699.340, www.hotelhasslerroma.com)* is steeped in prestige, refinement, and beauty. Paintings, silk tapestries, and wood paneling decorate the rooms with harmony and elegance, while dataports and other modern conveniences lend practicality. The rooftop restaurant is graced with magnificent views of Rome.

VIA VENETO

B: 52, 53, 63, 80, 95, 116, 119
M: A to Barberini

• SNAPSHOT •

The quarter gets its name from the street, Via Veneto, that snakes through what was once the Ludovisi family estate. In the 1870s, after Italian Unification, Villa Ludovisi went the way of many aristocratic palaces and gardens. It was sold off to speculators who built ostentatious *palazzi* in the area. By the 1950s and 1960s, the newly booming film industry gave an international patina to Via Veneto, and the quarter became the hot spot for celebrities. Cinecittà, Italy's Hollywood, welcomed U.S. productions in the 1950s, and their stars flocked to Via Veneto.

In 1960, Via Veneto was the central locale of Fellini's *La Dolce Vita*, a satire of the decadent lifestyles of the rich. The term *paparazzo* arose from the character of the same name in the film, a photographer who snapped pictures of the beautiful people. That same year, Luchino Visconti's *Rocco and His Brothers* and Michelangelo Antonioni's *L'Avventura* won awards. Rome is, of course, the centerpiece of Roberto Rossellini's *Rome, Open City*, his paean to the *Caput Mundi*. In more recent times, Cinecittà has seen a reawakening, with films like Nanni Moretti's *Caro Diario*, Roberto Benigni's *Life Is*

Beautiful, Anthony Minghella's *The Talented Mr. Ripley*, Martin Scorsese's *Gangs of New York*, and the blockbuster *Ocean's Twelve* shooting in studios or on location in the city.

PLACES TO SEE
Landmarks:

It's worth a visit to **Santa Maria della Vittoria (29)** *(Via XX Settembre 17, 06-42.74.05.71; hours: M–Sa 8:30AM–12PM, 3:30PM–6PM, Su 3:30PM–6PM)* just to see Bernini's sculpture *The Ecstasy of St. Teresa of Avila*. Italian artists have never shied away from putting rapture, religious or otherwise, on public display—and this St. Teresa is unquestionably in ecstasy. The 16th-century Spanish mystic is confronted by an angel with a golden spear, whether to protect or smite is not clear. Some say Teresa is experiencing divine joy; others claim it may be of a more somatic nature.

In **Piazza Barberini (30)**, ancients performed erotic Dionysian dances to welcome spring. Today Bernini's fabulous **Triton Fountain** makes up for the less than erotic atmosphere of traffic and exhaust fumes. The sea god

Triton sits on a shell, his fish tail curled beneath him, and blows water through a conch. Don't miss the small **Fountain of the Bees**, a drinking fountain in a corner of the piazza. Bees were the Barberini family symbol.

Via Veneto (31) winds its way gracefully from Piazza Barberini upward to **Porta Pinciana**, another arched gateway in the **Aurelian Wall** and an entrance to the Villa Borghese. A walk along the street once made glamorous by international film stars takes you past posh overpriced sidewalk cafés, opulent hotels, and the **Palazzo Margherita** *(Via Vittorio Veneto 119/a, 06-46.741)*, once a Ludovisi palazzo, now the U.S. Embassy. An uncharacteristically Goth spot along the tourist-crowded street is **Santa Maria della Concezione (32)** *(Via Veneto 27, 06-487.11.85, www.cappucciniviaveneto.it; hours: Church daily 7AM–12PM, 3PM–7PM, Crypt F–W 9AM–12PM, 3PM–6PM)*: in its underground crypt, the bones and skulls of thousands of Capuchin friars ornament the walls of several vaulted chapels.

Arts & Entertainment:
The **Palazzo Barberini (33)** *(Via delle Quattro Fontane 13, 06-32.810, www.galleriaborghese.it; hours: Tu–Su 8:30AM–7:30PM)*, built by Pope Urban VIII Barberini for his family in the early 17th century, houses the **Galleria Nazionale d'Arte Antica**, a significant museum. Works by Filippo Lippi, Caravaggio, and Hans Holbein the Younger are among many important pieces. *La Fornarina*, a famous painting believed to be of Raphael's mistress, is bold in its sensual coyness, with the mostly naked woman suggestively cupping her intimate parts with her hands.

PLACES TO EAT & DRINK
Where to Eat:

Dining around Via Veneto can be an expensive proposition but is often worth it. A romantic candlelight dinner, beneath a splendid cityscape, is simple and elegant at **La Terrazza dell'Eden (34)** (€€€) *(Via Ludovisi 49, 06-47.81.21, www.hotel-eden.it; hours: daily 7AM–10:30AM, 12:30PM–2:30PM, 7:30PM–10:30PM)*. The excellent Tuscan restaurant **Papà Baccus (35)** (€€-€€€) *(Via Toscana 36, 06-42.74.28.08, www.papabaccus.com; call for hours)* serves authentic dishes using products shipped in from Tuscany. The service makes you feel like you're their best guest.

Sleek, chic, and ultramodern, **Moma (37)** (€€) *(Via San Basilio 42-43, 06-42.01.17.98; call for hours)* does a revision of traditional Italian and foreign cuisines. For good, inexpensive Chinese food, **Jasmine (38)** (€) *(Via Sicilia 45, 06-42.88.49.83; call for hours)* is the answer.

Bars & Nightlife:

The upstairs tearoom **Sala degli Angeli, Café de Paris (40)** *(Via Vittorio Veneto 91, 06-42.01.10.90; hours: Su–Th 8AM–1AM, F–Sa 8AM–2AM)* is a chic place to be seen, with the recent remodeling of the place ratcheting up its hipness factor. The pastries are delectable, and there's a good selection of fine teas. In the 1950s and 1960s, Ava Gardner, Richard Burton, and Burt Lancaster (not together) were patrons of the bar **Doney (41)** *(Via Vittorio Veneto 145, 06-47.08.28.05; hours: daily 8AM–1AM)*. It's hip and hot once again. If the candles and chandeliers are too much for you, claim a spot on one of the sidewalk sofas and watch the beautiful people go by. Andy Warhol quotes deck the walls at **San Marco (42)** *(Via Sardegna 38d, 06-42.82.48.93; call for hours)*, a wine bar that doubles as restaurant/pizzeria/grill. Rustic with long cherrywood tables and greengrocer's cabinets, it also has a patio outside. It's a pleasant place, and every once in a while it welcomes a party in swing.

WHERE TO SHOP

Via Veneto is the place to go for conservative, refined clothing. Classic Italian knitwear seems to weather the decades: you might find the perfect piece at **Albertina (43)** *(Via Lazio 20, 06-488.58.76)*. Well-to-do gentlemen have been going to **Brioni (44)** *(Via Barberini 79-81, 06-485.855, www.brioni.com)* forever for the perfect three-piece suit. **Aston (45)** *(Via Boncompagni 27, 06-42.82.66.47)* carries designer fabrics, unique both in texture and print. Part flea market, part antique shop, **Michel Harem (46)** *(Via Sistina 137, 06-474.64.66)* carries eclectic curios and wacky *follie*.

WHERE TO STAY

Extravagant, sensual, and deliciously inviting, the **Aleph Hotel (47)** (€€€) *(Via di San Basilio 15, 06-42.29.01, www.boscolohotels.com)* plays a game between the color red—on floors, chair coverings, drapes, and lights—and white-and-black schemes. New York architect Adam Tihany designed the place to reflect the contradictions inherent in Rome—purity and decadence, heaven and hell, the divine and the devilish. The rooms themselves are blissful. Blue and ivory hues are accented by lighting fixtures of Murano glass.

VILLA BORGHESE

B: 52, 53, 88, 95, 116, 490, 495

• SNAPSHOT •

Many of Rome's aristocratic families produced popes, who in turn gave further clout to the clans, often build-ing majestic palaces on lands they already owned or soon bought. Camillo Borghese became Pope Paul V (1605–1621), ringing in an era of enormous power and profit for his family. Nephew Scipione, an aficionado of the arts who soon became a cardinal, built the Villa Borghese on the family's vineyards and bought much of the surrounding land. It was a dramatic statement and a model to which other prominent families looked when constructing their own estates: Villa Ludovisi, Villa Farnese, and Villa Doria Pamphili, among others. Today, the state-owned Villa Borghese is a superb public park, replete with museums, gardens, lakes, arbors, fountains, neoclassical temples, statues, and a plethora of jogging paths and picnic grounds. Centrally located, it offers Romans and visitors alike a respite from city living, all within walking distance of the cheerful chaos. Rental bikes make it easier to cover the grounds *(for rentals, see page 14).*

PLACES TO SEE
Landmarks:

The ★**VILLA BORGHESE** is the perfect place to recover if you've OD'd on culture and the city. It's great for jogging, boating, strolling, or picnicking. If you've not had your fill of art and history, it also contains great museums and a zoo. Along your walks, don't miss the **Temple of Diana (48)**, a round, open-air neoclassical structure between **Porta Pinciana** and Piazza di Siena. Many of the structures were made in the Baroque period to look like ancient temples. The **Temple of Aesculapius (49)**, in the arti-

ficial lake of the *Giardino del Lago*, is a neoclassical monument in Ionian style. The **Bioparco (50)** *(Viale del Giardino Zoologico, 06-360.82.11, www.bioparco.it; hours: daily 9:30AM–5/6PM)*—a zoo, conservation center, and zoological museum (with sections on biodiversity and habitats of the Lazio Province)—is in the northeast corner of the park.

Arts & Entertainment:

The hedonistic Cardinal Scipione Borghese, who concocted the villa and park, was a patron of the arts. His palazzo is now the ★**GALLERIA BORGHESE (51)** *(Piazzale Scipione Borghese 5, 06-328.10, www.galleriaborghese.it; hours: Tu–Su 8:30AM–7:30PM)*, which houses the spectacular private Borghese collection. The ground floor is dedicated to sculpture, while paintings are displayed on the upper floor. Some of the highlights are Titian's *Sacred and Profane Love*, Bernini's *Apollo and Daphne*, and Canova's *Pauline Borghese* (Napoleon's sister, Prince Camillo Borghese's wife). When Camillo saw the nearly-naked marble *Pauline*, he locked up the statue, forbidding even Canova to see it once it was done. Caravaggio, in his painting *David with the Head of Goliath*, did a self-portrait as the decapitated Goliath: it revealed his terror at possibly being guillotined for murdering a tennis opponent; he was eventually pardoned for the crime.

The **National Gallery of Modern Art (52)** *(Viale delle Belle Arti 131, 06-32.29.81, www.gnam.arti.beniculturali. it/gnamco.htm)*, housed in a beautiful neoclassical palazzo, is a collection of 19th- and 20th-century art. It includes Italian artists such as Canova, De Chirico, Morandi, and Modigliani, as well as foreign masters such as Cézanne, Van Gogh, Rodin, and Klimt.

The **Villa Giulia (53)** *(Piazzale di Villa Giulia 9, 06-322.65.71)*, a museum covering pre-Roman epochs, is the most significant Etruscan museum in Italy. The Etruscans, an ancient civilization whose origins are unknown, ruled Rome in the 7th–6th century BC. By the 1st century BC, they had been integrated into the Roman empire.

PLACES TO EAT & DRINK
Where to Eat:

It's worth a trek to the northern border of Villa Borghese to the exclusive Aldrovandi Palace Hotel, where one of Italy's great chefs, Alfonso Iaccarino, opened his Roman restaurant **Baby (54)** (€€€€) *(Via Ulisse Aldrovandi 15, 06-321.61.26, www.aldrovandi.com; call for hours)*. Zen-like, overlooking a garden, it's an incredible dining experience. A creative spin on traditional Roman cuisine combines with the chef's own classics, like *bucatini* with baby octopus.

Bars & Nightlife:

Well into the morning hours, the **Piazza di Siena Art Caffè (55)** *(Viale del Galoppatoio 33, 06-36.00.65.78; hours: Tu–Su 7:30PM–3AM)* is a happening place. From June to August, it's hopping with live music, performances, art installations, and fashion shows. In winter the whole shebang simply moves into the Villa Borghese car park.

WHERE TO SHOP

While in the **Galleria Borghese (51)**, check out the Galleria Borghese Museum Shop (56) *(P.zale del Museo Borghese 5, 06-855.73.77)*, which offers museum reproductions, jewelry, books, and a wide variety of gifts.

chapter 3

QUIRINALE/TREVI

ESQUILINO & MONTI

SAN LORENZO

QUIRINALE/TREVI
ESQUILINO & MONTI
SAN LORENZO

Places to See:

1. TREVI FOUNTAIN ★
2. Santa Maria in Trivio
3. Via della Pilotta
4. Palazzo del Quirinale
5. Piazza della Repubblica
6. Terme di Diocleziano
7. San Luca National Academy of Art
8. Pasta Museum
9. Palazzo Colonna
10. Museo Nazionale di Roma: Terme di Diocleziano
11. Santa Maria degli Angeli
12. Aula Ottagona
13. Teatro dell'Opera
14. Scuderie del Quirinale
15. Palazzo delle Esposizioni
27. SANTA MARIA MAGGIORE ★
28. SAN PIETRO IN VINCOLI ★
29. Domus Aurea
30. Parco del Colle Oppio
31. Galleria Termini/GATE
46. San Lorenzo fuori le Mura
47. Galleria Pino Casagrande

Places to Eat & Drink:

16. L'Antica Birreria Peroni
17. Trattoria Tritone
18. Il Gelato di San Crispino
19. Trimani
32. Agata e Romeo
33. F.I.S.H.
34. Hasekura
35. Al Vino Al Vino
36. Bohemien
37. Fiddler's Elbow
48. Il Dito e la Luna
49. Arancia Blu
50. Pommidoro
51. Tram Tram
52. Ferrazza

Where to Shop:

20. Feltrinelli International
21. Trimani
22. Il Giardino di Domenico Persiani
26. Termini Train Station
38. Panella
39. La Bottega del Cioccolato
40. Le Gallinelle
53. Claudio Sano

★ *Top Picks*

54. Myriam B

Where to Stay:

QUIRINALE/TREVI

*B: Quirinale—H, 40, 64, 70, 170, routes along
Via del Nazionale; Trevi—52, 53, 61, 62, 63, 71, 80,
95, 116, routes along Via del Corso and Via del Tritone;
Repubblica—36, 60, 61, 62, 64, 84, 90,
170, 175, 492, 649, 910*

M: A to Repubblica

• SNAPSHOT •

Rome was built on seven hills: Quirinale, Viminale, Esquilino, Celio, Campidoglio or Capitolino, Palatino, and Aventino. Other city hills—the Gianicolo, Colle Oppio, and Velia—are not listed among the official seven. The Quirinale was residential during the Empire and the first to be rediscovered and developed during the Renaissance. Whoever had enough money to get away from the insalubrious low ground moved up to the hills. In the late 16th century, the papacy moved to the Palazzo Quirinale, its summer residence at the top of the hill, away from the smelly, malaria-infested Tiber. Aristocratic families, such as the Colonna and Aldobrandini, built palaces on the hill as well. Italian Unification in 1870 marked the end of papal rule. Rome was made the capital of the new nation, and the papacy vacated the Palazzo Quirinale, which became the royal palace and later the presidential palace.

PLACES TO SEE
Landmarks:

The overpowering ★TREVI FOUNTAIN (1) takes up most of the space of the small Piazza di Trevi. Atop large boulders, marble statues depict the sea god Neptune riding in a chariot pulled by two sea horses. Two tritons manage them, one sea horse ruly, the other calm—the two opposing aspects of the ocean. Salubrity and Abundance oversee the scene from the background. In niches above the fountain, along the back wall, are statues memorializing the history of the 15.5-mile-long conduit, the Acqua Vergine, that brought water to the Quirinale. One represents Rome, the terminus of the canal; the other, the virgin (for whom the aqueduct was named), who

showed the Roman soldiers the spring from which the water was drawn. The modern Trevi myth is that if you toss a coin into the fountain, you'll return to Rome—a practice memorialized in the 1954 film *Three Coins in the Fountain*. Once a week the basin is cleaned and the coins collected and donated to the Italian Red Cross.

Rome is full of playful, quirky spots. Around the corner from the Trevi Fountain, **Santa Maria in Trivio (2)** *(P.za dei Crociferi 49, 06-678.96.45; hours: daily 8AM–12PM, 4PM–7:30PM)* looks like just a façade, as though it were glued onto the building behind it. It even has fake windows! One of the more delightful spots in Rome is just a few streets away, the **Via della Pilotta (3)**. Its succession of romantic arches takes you back to days when illicit lovers, caped and hooded, furtively ran through the arcades to secret assignations.

Wind your way via staircases and sloping streets up the hill to **Palazzo del Quirinale (4)** *(P.za del Quirinale, 06-469.91, www.quirinale.it; hours: Su 8:30AM–12PM)* where, in the piazza fronting the palace, you'll find Roman copies of 5th-century BC Greek statues of the brothers Castor and Pollux. Known for their equestrian abilities, they are always represented, as here, with lively horses. The **Palazzo del Quirinale (4)** was built in the 16th century by Pope Gregory XIII as a summer residence for the pope and his entourage.

Sober, dignified 19th-century **Piazza della Repubblica (5)** was built on what was the *exedra*, the semicircular recess, of the Baths of Diocletian. It was constructed during the 19th-century redevelopment that marked Rome's new status as capital of Italy. Elegant colonnades encircle the piazza and the central fountain with four bronze nymphs astride various water animals. The naked nymphs created a scandal in 1901 when they were unveiled.

Across the piazza are the Baths of Diocletian, or **Terme di Diocleziano (6)** *(Viale E. de Nicola 79, 06-39.96. 77.00; hours: Tu–Su 9AM–7:45PM)*. Built by the forced labor of 40,000 Christians, the grounds included gardens, galleries, concert halls, libraries, and the bath-house, which held 3,000 people at a time. After the Ostrogoths demolished the aqueducts, the baths were abandoned in 538, and ten centuries later Pope Pius IV commissioned the 86-year-old Michelangelo to convert the ruins into a church, **Santa Maria degli Angeli (11)** *(see page 81)*. With the city's restoration projects of 2000, the Terme became part of the **Museo Nazionale di Roma (10)** *(see page 81)*.

Arts & Entertainment:

The gallery at the **San Luca National Academy of Art (7)** *(P.za dell'Accademia di San Luca 77, 06-679.88.50, www.accademiasanluca.it/whoweare.html; call for hours)* contains significant work by famous artists, such as Raphael and Canova. For a change of pace, check out the **Pasta Museum (8)** *(P.za Scanderbeg 117, 06-699.11.19, www.pastainmuseum.com; hours: daily 9:30AM–5:30PM).*

 It contains whatever you want to know about pasta, and more—history, production, and pasta-themed art. Take Via di San Vincenzo, which eventually becomes the beautiful Via della Pilotta, to **Palazzo Colonna (9)** *(Via della Pilotta 17, 06-679.43.62, www.galleriacolonna.it; hours: Sa 9AM–1PM).* The Colonna family mansion was begun in the 15th century by Pope Martin V Colonna but finished in the 18th century. The family's art collection is open to the public in the art gallery, from where you can see the lovely private gardens and ruins of the Temple of Serapis.

The museum at the Baths of Diocletian, **Museo Nazionale di Roma: Terme di Diocleziano (10)** *(Via Enrico de Nicola 79, 06-39.96.77.00; hours: Tu–Su 9AM–7:45PM)*, affords a marvelous view of the ancient Roman site and the central cloister, restored by Michelangelo. Fragments of the baths are in **Santa Maria degli Angeli (11)** *(P.za della Repubblica, 06-488.08.12, www.santamariadegliangeliroma.it; hours: daily 7AM–6:30PM)*, the magnificent church designed by Michelangelo. The restored **Aula Ottagona (12)** *(Via Romita 8, 06-39.96.77.00; hours: M–Sa 9:30AM–1:30PM, 2:30PM–5PM)* now exhibits large classical sculptures.

If you haven't had enough drama, take in a great Italian operatic tragedy at **Teatro dell'Opera (13)** *(P.za Beniamino Gigli 7, 06-*  48.16.02.55, www.operaroma.it; box office hours: Tu–Sa 9AM–5PM, Su 9AM–1:30PM; tickets online: www. amitsrl.it)*. Or check out the old stables and coach house of the presidential palace, **Scuderie del Quirinale (14)** *(Via XXIV Maggio 16, 06-39.96.75.00, www.scuderie quirinale.it; hours: Su–Th 10AM–8PM, F–Sa 10AM–10:30PM)*, revamped and turned into a cultural center and exhibition space by architect Gae Aulenti. Another arts center in the area, **Palazzo delle Esposizioni (15)** *(Via Nazionale 194, 06-48.94.11, www.palaexpo.it; call for hours)*, is an exciting forum for contemporary art and photography.

PLACES TO EAT & DRINK
Where to Eat:

Whether or not you love beer, **L'Antica Birreria Peroni (16)** (€) *(Via San Marcello 19, 06-679.53.10, www.anticabirreriaperoni.it; hours: M–Sa 12PM–12AM)* is an experience in social eating. The communal seating integrates you with the Roman beer-hall scene. The Tyrolean menu is hearty, and the beers are exceptional. Great service, great food, and a friendly welcome greet you at **Trattoria Tritone (17)** (€€) *(Via dei Maroniti 1, 06-679.81.81, www.trattoriatritone.com; hours: daily 12PM–11PM)*, where you can hobnob with Italian journalists. **Il Gelato di San Crispino (18)** (€) *(Via della Panetteria 42, 06-679.39.24, www.ilgelatodisancrispino.it; hours: Su–Th 12PM–12:30AM, F–Sa 12PM–1:30AM, closed Tu in autumn/winter)* is possibly the best ice cream shop in all Rome. The ingredients are so fresh and seasonal that some of the flavors come and go in less than a month.

Bars & Nightlife:

The oldest wine shop in Rome has a wine bar next door: cozy **Trimani (19)** *(Via Cernaia 37b, 06-446.96.30, www.trimani.com; call for hours)*, near the Baths of Diocletian, offers a wide variety of wines and good food.

WHERE TO SHOP

One of Italy's largest chain bookstores, **Feltrinelli International (20)** *(Via Vittorio Emanuele Orlando 84, 06-482.78.78, www.lafeltrinelli.it)* carries a large selection of books, CDs, and DVDs in the original language, including English. Get lost browsing through the shelves. The selection of wines and gourmet foods at **Trimani (21)** *(Via Goito 20, 06-446.96.61, www.trimani.com)* is fantastic. You can sample the olive oil before purchasing. A jar of truffle paste, a loaf of bread, and a bottle of Chianti—all are the ingredients for a picnic at the Baths of Diocletian or the **Aula Ottagona (12)**. For just about any fabulous ceramic you can imagine, **Il Giardino di Domenico Persiani (22)** *(Via Torino 92, 06-488.38.86)* will fill you with delight. Ready-made tiles, special-order pieces, copies of famous statues—you could spend an afternoon browsing through the garden.

WHERE TO STAY

Spacious and classy, **Hotel Exedra (23)** (€€€) *(P.za della Repubblica 47, 06-48.93.81, www.boscolohotels.com)* integrates the ancient and the modern. Glass floors in meeting rooms allow viewing of ancient ruins, while the atrium is airy and light. Rooms, too, are spacious. The lobby of the **St. Regis Grand (24)** (€€€€) *(Via Vittorio Emanuele Orlando 3, 06-47.091, www.starwoodhotels.com)* lives up to the *grand* in its name. Its elegant Murano chandeliers set the tone, and every room has frescoes above the bed. **Residenza Cellini (25)** (€€) *(Via Modena 5, 06-47.82.52.04, www.residenzacellini.it)*, a B&B run by two brothers and a sister, has large rooms with hardwood floors, high ceilings, and bathrooms with hydromassage showers and heated towel racks.

ESQUILINO & MONTI

B: Santa Maria Maggiore—16, 70, 71, 714;
San Pietro in Vincoli—75, 84, 117

M: A or B to Termini; B to Cavour;
A to Vittorio Emanuele

• SNAPSHOT •

The area of Esquilino and Monti once included the most exclusive and most wretched of Rome's inhabitants. Esquilino Hill, southeast of the Quirinale, was home to the wealthiest families of ancient and papal Rome, while Monti, the low, swampy slum between the two hills, was left to the urban poor. Today Monti is one of the trendiest areas of Rome, with some great restaurants, numerous interesting shops, and designers and craftsmen who ply their trade with the passion of their spiritual forefathers.

Esquilino has become Rome's experiment in multiculturalism. In a city not especially known for diversity, recent immigrants have made this area a colorful mix of cultures from many continents. Ethiopians, Eritreans, Chinese, and Italians coexist and thrive with shops and businesses exchanging services and clients. One of Rome's most magnificent churches is located in Esquilino: Santa Maria Maggiore is superb, both architecturally and artistically. San Pietro in Vincoli, another must-see, contains Michelangelo's *Moses*.

PLACES TO SEE
Landmarks:

One of Rome's great basilicas, ★SANTA MARIA MAGGIORE (27) *(P.za di Santa Maria Maggiore, 06-48.31.95; hours: daily 7AM–7PM)* is an architectural marvel, success-

TOP PICK!

fully integrating several different styles—Romanesque, medieval, Renaissance, and Baroque—with front and rear façades on two large piazzas. The legend of its creation is that the Virgin Mary came to Pope Liberius in a dream, instructing him to build a church in a place where he found snow. On August 5, 356, it snowed on the Esquiline. Seeing this as a miracle, Pope Liberius obeyed her exhortation. In a yearly service commemorating the event, white rose petals are dropped from the church's ceiling. The interior is amazing. Gilded coffered ceilings; opulent chapels; magnificent detailing in marble, bronze, and porphyry; and spectacular mosaics are among the wonders of Santa Maria Maggiore, which is one of the four major basilicas of Rome (along with St. Peter's in the Vatican, San Giovanni in Laterano, and San Paolo Fuori le Mura).

The chains binding St. Peter in Jerusalem and while he was in the Mamertine Prison near the Roman Forum, *(see page 129)* are the relics that give ★SAN PIETRO IN VINCOLI (28) *(P.za di San Pietro in Vincoli 4A, 06-488.28.65; hours: daily 7AM–12:30PM, 3:30PM–7PM, Oct–Mar til 6PM)* its name ("St. Peter in Chains") and are displayed below the high altar. Legend has it that

TOP PICK!

when the chains were placed next to each other, they miraculously fused together. Originally built in the 5th century, the church has undergone many touch-ups and restorations. It is best known for **Michelangelo's masterpiece, *Moses***, sculpted for the tomb of Pope Julius II. The seated figure instills reverence and embodies wisdom, fortitude, honor, conviction, and inner strength. Interestingly, the horns on his head are the result of a flawed translation from the Old Testament. Instead of horns, they're supposed to be beams of light. In addition to *Moses*, Michelangelo is also believed to have finished the statues of *Rachel* and *Leah* before having to abandon this project to begin work on the Sistine Chapel.

Emperor Nero is said to have set fire to Rome in AD 64, perhaps to grab most of the Oppian Hill and build the **Domus Aurea (29)** *(Via della Domus Aurea, 06-39.96.77.00; reserve ahead; hours: Tu–F 10AM–4PM)*. Encircled by man-made lakes and forests, his "Golden House," a palace fit for Nero's megalomania and debauchery, was 25 times as big as the Colosseum and was covered in gold outside and inlaid with jewels and mother-of-pearl inside. The ruins of the **Domus Aurea (29)** are situated in the lovely park on the Oppian side of the Esquilino. The **Parco del Colle Oppio (30)** is as high as the top floors of the Colosseum; thus, the ancient amphitheatre seems to rise up so close you could almost touch it.

Arts & Entertainment:

Galleria Termini/GATE (31) *(Termini Station, Ala Mazzoniana, Via Giolitti 34, by gate/binario 24)* exhibits modern art and photography, providing a great way to pass the time while waiting for your train.

PLACES TO EAT & DRINK
Where to Eat:

Agata e Romeo (32) (€€€€) *(Via Carlo Alberto 45, 06-446.61.15, www.agataeromeo.it; call for hours, closed Sa–Su)* is on everyone's list: Roman haute cuisine with classic underpinnings. Eating is a trip here, the comfortable but subdued décor bowing out to focus the senses on the food. Sheep's milk cheese tart with pear sauce, celery and oxtail terrine, pasta with saffron cheese, Icelandic cod—they're all distinctive and excellent.

F.I.S.H. (33) (€€) *(Via dei Serpenti 16, 06-47.82.49.62, www.f-i-s-h.it; call for hours, closed M)* stands for Fine International Seafood House, and that's exactly what it is. From sushi and sashimi to the most delicate, thin fish *carpaccios*, the menu is a fantasy from the sea with Mediterranean, Asian, and Pacific Rim cuisine. A restaurant that's made its mark in the Monti area with exceptional Japanese food is **Hasekura (34) (€€-€€€)** *(Via dei Serpenti 27, 06-48.36.48; hours: daily 12PM–2:30PM, 7PM–10:30PM)*, one of the hottest eateries around.

Bars & Nightlife:

Al Vino Al Vino (35) *(Via dei Serpenti 19, 06-48.58.03; hours: daily 10:30AM–2:30PM, 5PM–1AM)* is mostly a wine bar frequented by a multiculti crowd, a great place to check out the local hipsters. It has a good selection of wines, especially sweet wines *(passiti)*, and a variety of *grappas*. The crowd at **Bohemien (36)** *(Via degli Zingari 36, 06-97.60.13.96; call for hours)* is casual, friendly, and mostly gay; the bar is unpretentious and doubles as a design, art, and photography bookstore. Romans adore **Fiddler's Elbow (37)** *(Via dell'Olmata 43, 06-487.21.10, www.thefiddlerselbow.com; hours: daily 5PM–2AM)*, an old Irish pub whose fiddlers, all volunteer musicians, might inspire you to dance an impromptu *céil'*.

WHERE TO SHOP

On the north side of the Esquilino, not far from the Baths of Diocletian, is the **Termini Train Station (26)** *(P.za del Cinquecento, www.romatermini.it)*. In the city's perennial attempts to brighten the seedy area, a mini-mall was created here in 2000, with shops, boutiques, bookstores, eateries, and an art gallery *(see page 87)*, as well as a 24-hour supermarket. Despite this resurrection, the train station is still to be avoided at night.

With more than 80 varieties of bread, **Panella (38)** *(Via Merulana 54-55, 06-487.23.44; hours: M–F 8AM–1:30PM, 5:30PM–8PM, Sa–Su 8AM–1:30PM)* has more than enough varieties to satisfy your bread cravings. From Pompeian doughs to crusty baguettes to pizzas to pastries, they're all delicious. If chocolate is your thing,

La Bottega del Cioccolato (39) *(Via Leonina 82, 06-482.14.73, www.labottegadelcioccolato.it)* is an obligatory stop. The dark chocolate, 90% cocoa (Brazilian), is amazing; but the truffles, peppermint chocolate bars, and fruit and nut combinations are all divine.

Fashionistas, don't miss Le Gallinelle (40) *(Via del Boschetto 76, 06-488.101, www.legallinelle.it)*, a vintage designer fashion boutique that now carries its own creations. Owner Wilma Silvestri makes draped evening gowns, kicky skirts, sundresses, and lots more. A vintage Gucci bag might be just what you wanted for a night out in Monti.

WHERE TO STAY

Radisson SAS (43) (€€-€€€) *(Via Filippo Turati 171, 06-44.48.41, www.radissonsas.com)* is the cat's meow in high-tech, minimalist living. Often a venue for fashion and film shoots, it includes a state-of-the-art gym, rooftop pool, spa, the ultra-modern restaurant **Sette**, and a cocktail bar, **Zest**. For studio or apartment rentals, Residenza Monti (44) (€-€€) *(Via dei Serpenti 15, 06-481.57.36, www.therelaxinghotels.com)* provides a quiet respite from the buzz of the Monti district. The rooms are rather small but comfortable and accommodating. Bare beams and iron beds give Antica Locanda (45) (€) *(Via del Boschetto 84, 06-48.48.94, www.antica-locanda.com)* a special charm, while the roof garden of this old palazzo looks onto ancient ruins.

SAN LORENZO

B: 71, 204, 310, 492, 649
M: A or B to Termini

• SNAPSHOT •

San Lorenzo is a lively district with a left-wing, antifascist past. Created in the late 19th century, the working-class neighborhood suffered from substandard living conditions, and the populace rebelled. By the 1920s, they were battling fascists in the streets; during Mussolini's era San Lorenzo became a meeting place for antifascists. Ironically, it was heavily bombed during World War II; consequently the buildings are post-1945 constructions. Currently, the district is fascinating because of the artistic passion and cultural diversity of its inhabitants; it is home to a young generation of artists. Residents, along with students from the nearby university, La Sapienza, and visitors coming to experience the innovative and creative energy of the district, keep the bars, clubs, and eateries open all night. The old Cerere pasta factory has been converted into artists' lofts. With

the influx of young designers, hip restaurants and bars have followed, sharing the streets with traditional, inexpensive working-class trattorias. San Lorenzo has no real landmarks of note; rather, it is interesting because of its creative life force.

PLACES TO SEE
Landmarks:
La Sapienza *(Piazzale Aldo Moro 5, 06-499.11)* is the largest university in Europe, and its main campus, **Città Universitaria**, is just north of the San Lorenzo district. The university's architecture is typical of the fascist aesthetic of the 1930s, when it was built. At the quarter's northern tip on Piazzale del Verano, the basilica of **San Lorenzo fuori le Mura (46)** *(Piazzale del Verano 3, 06-49.15.11; hours: Apr–Sept daily 7:30AM–12:30PM, Oct–Mar daily 7:30AM–12:30PM, 3PM–7PM)* was originally a gift of Emperor Constantine to house the tomb of St. Lawrence. Byzantine icons, created with pieces of marble in the Greek tradition, lack the brilliance evident in Roman mosaics made of glass.

Arts & Entertainment:
San Lorenzo has increasingly become a hotbed of contemporary art. Blending into the ethos of the neighborhood, **Galleria Pino Casagrande (47)** *(Via degli Ausoni 7a, 06-446.34.80; call for hours)*, in the textile connoisseur's home, displays his art collection. Furniture by Mies van der Rohe, Le Corbusier, Ettore Sottsass, and others blends with the antiqui-ties and contemporary art that Casagrande has collected, including works by Sol Le Witt, Donald Judd, and Julian Opie.

PLACES TO EAT & DRINK
Where to Eat:

San Lorenzo would be worth a visit if only to taste the fabulous southern Italian cuisine at **Il Dito e la Luna (48)** (€€) *(Via dei Sabelli 51, 06-494.07.26; call for hours)*. Delicate flavors blend to burst on the palate. Fennel salad with black olives and oranges—yum! Leave room for the delectable chocolate soufflé. **Arancia Blu (49)** (€€) *(Via dei Latini 55-65, 06-445.41.05; hours: daily 8PM–12AM)* has become  famous for its mouthwatering vegetarian food. Artichokes on a bed of creamed chickpeas, nut ravioli with rosemary and Parmesan sauce, and pasta with truffles are some of the gourmet creations.

Filmmaker Pier Paolo Pasolini, who loved the working-class San Lorenzo neighborhood, was a regular at **Pommidoro (50)** (€€) *(P.za dei Sanniti 44, 06-445.26.92; call for hours)*. Local artists continue to cross its threshold, as well as soccer stars from the Roma team. The *spaghetti alla carbonara* is great, and the place is known for its grilled meats. Friendly and relaxed, the owner might be prompted to tell you stories about the neighborhood.

One of the first eateries to open in San Lorenzo, **Tram Tram (51)** (€€) *(Via dei Reti 44, 06-49.04.16; hours: Tu–Su 12:30PM–3:30PM, 7:30PM–11:30PM)* continues to be exceptionally good. Beans with chicory, swordfish with anchovies, broccoli and clam pasta—the combinations are unique and delicious. The place gets its name from the neighborhood tramline; old train parts serve as booths and wine racks.

Bars & Nightlife:

The wine bar **Ferrazza (52)** *(Via dei Volsci 59, 06-49.05.06; hours: M–Sa 6PM–2AM)* is one of the city's best drinking spots, a place for people-watching among the crowds of young artists, local artisans, and students. It has a selection of fabulous cocktail snacks in the early evening. The cavernlike interior is brick-lined and pleasant.

WHERE TO SHOP

The working-class roots of San Lorenzo can be seen in the artisan workshops, open-air markets, and neighborly relations among the locals. The leather goods at Claudio Sano (53) *(Largo degli Osci 67a, 06-446.92.84, www.claudiosano.it)*, all handmade on the premises, are beautifully crafted from carefully treated and finished leather. Imaginative designs for handbags, briefcases, sandals, belts, and other products assure the unique look of these goods. The creative jewelry designs of Myriam Bottazzi, available at her showroom Myriam B (54) *(Via dei Volsci 75, 06-44.36.13.05, www.myriamb.it; hours: Tu–Sa 11AM–1PM, 5PM–8PM, Su–M 5PM–8PM)* have become legendary. They make a statement without being excessive. Fashion designers Romeo Gigli and Martine Sitbon are among her clients.

chapter 4

LATERAN
CELIO
CARACALLA
OUTSKIRTS OFF CARACALLA

LATERAN
CELIO
CARACALLA
OUTSKIRTS OFF CARACALLA

Places to See:

1. San Giovanni in Laterano
2. Piazza di San Giovanni in Laterano
3. Scala Santa
4. Santa Croce in Gerusalemme
5. Porta Maggiore
6. Santi Quattro Coronati
7. Museum of Musical Instruments
8. Historic Museum of the Liberation of Rome
15. San Clemente
16. Santi Giovanni e Paolo
17. Clivio di Scauro
18. San Gregorio Magno
19. Villa Celimontana
20. Santa Maria in Domnica
21. Santo Stefano Rotondo
22. Galleria Arte e Pensieri
23. Antiquarium Comunale
25. Galleria SALES
37. Santa Balbina
38. Santi Nereo e Achilleo
39. San Sisto Vecchio

40. San Cesareo
41. San Giovanni a Porta Latina
42. San Giovanni in Oleo
43. BATHS OF CARACALLA ★
44. Columbarium of Pomponius Hylas
45. Scipio Tomb
46. Porta San Sebastiano
47. Wall Museum
48. Arch of Drusus
49. Gruppo Storico Romano
50. Appian Way
51. Catacombs of San Callisto
52. Catacombs of San Sebastiano
53. Fosse Ardeatine
54. Catacombs of Domitilla
55. Tomb of Cecilia Metella

Places to Eat & Drink:

9. La Tana dei Golosi
10. Isidoro
11. Hosteria degli Artisti
24. Crab
26. Le Naumachie
27. Centrum
28. Café Café

★ *Top Picks*

95

29. Coming Out

Where to Shop:

Where to Stay:

LATERAN

B: P.za San Giovanni—16, 81, 85, 87, 186, 650, 850;
Santa Croce in Gerualsemme—16, 81, 649, 810

M: A to Manzoni or San Giovanni; B to Colosseo

• SNAPSHOT •

The area of Lateran lies between the Celian and Esquiline hills. It was named after a wealthy family, the Laterani. Today the Lateran is known for the basilica of Rome, San Giovanni in Laterano (St. John Lateran), which was founded in the 4th century AD by Emperor Constantine. He had a vision before going into battle: Christ came to him and told him to put a Christian symbol on his soldiers' shields. Constantine won the battle against Maxentius, thereby becoming emperor. He converted to the new religion and immediately legalized Christianity, forbidding the persecution of its followers. Most people in Rome, however, were still non-Christians, so he chose a location away from the center of the city to build a basilica—in the Lateran. It was less likely to agitate the pagans, but was still within the walls of Rome.

PLACES TO SEE
Landmarks:

The focus of this quarter is **San Giovanni in Laterano (1)** *(P.za*

San Giovanni in Laterano 4, 06-69.88.64.33/52; hours:
Church daily 7AM–6:30PM, Cloister daily 9AM–6PM,
Museum M–Sa 9AM–1PM), the cathedral of Rome. It was
built by Emperor Constantine in the early 4th century
over the barracks of Emperor Maxentius's bodyguards,
thus symbolically proclaiming Constantine's victory
over Maxentius and the victory of Christianity over
paganism. Architecturally modified over the years, the
present church dates from the 17th century. It is one of
the four major basilicas of Rome, together with St.
Peter's in the Vatican, Santa Maria Maggiore, and San
Paolo Fuori le Mura. Its façade, with 15 stunningly
enormous statues standing on the pediment atop the
church, makes the basilica recognizable from a distance.
Inside, the statues of the twelve apostles were sculpted
by Borromini.

The cathedral's **Baptistery** and the **Lateran Palace**, the old
papal residence, are on the **Piazza di San Giovanni in
Laterano (2)**, facing another Egyptian obelisk, the oldest
and tallest in Rome. The profusion of Egyptian obelisks
in Rome attests to the military might of ancient Rome:
they were highly prized war trophies because of their
power in Egypt as symbols of the pharaohs' immortali-
ty and divinity. Every May 1, labor unions celebrate
International Workers' Day on the piazza with a free
rock concert.

On the eastern edge of the piazza is what is thought to
be a relic brought to Rome in 326 from the Holy Land
by St. Helena, mother of Emperor Constantine. The

Scala Santa (3) *(P.za di San Giovanni in Laterano 14, 06-772.66.41; hours: daily 6:30AM–12PM, 3PM–6PM)*, the Holy Staircase, is comprised of 28 marble stairs said to be the very steps Christ climbed in Pontius Pilate's palace in Jerusalem before his crucifixion. No foot is allowed to touch them, so they are covered by wooden boards which pious Christians ascend on their knees.

In the eastern sector of the Lateran, **Santa Croce in Gerusalemme (4)** *(P.za di Santa Croce in Gerusalemme 12, 06-701.47.69, www.basilicasantacroce.it; hours: daily 7AM–12PM, 3PM–6:30PM)* (Holy Cross in Jerusalem) was part of St. Helena's palace. Built in 320 to house relics of the Crucifixion that she was said to have brought back from Jerusalem, it was redone in the 18th century. It houses what are supposed to be pieces of Christ's cross (the "True Cross"), a nail from the cross, two thorns from the Crown of Thorns, and the finger that doubting St. Thomas purportedly put into Christ's wound.

A few streets to the north, **Porta Maggiore (5)** *(P.za di Porta Maggiore)*, with its two arches, was the entry point for aqueducts carrying water into the city. The original acqueduct, Aqua Claudia, was built by Emperor Claudius in AD 52. **Santi Quattro Coronati (6)** *(Via dei Santi Quattro Coronati 20, 06-70.47.54.27, www.santiquattrocoronati.org; hours: daily 6:30AM–12PM, 3:30PM–7:30PM)*, "Four Crowned Saints," is a convent dedicated to four Christian soldiers executed for refusing to renounce their religion. The 13th-century frescoes in the Chapel of St. Sylvester tell the story of Emperor Constantine suffering from the plague. Be sure not to miss the cloister *(ring the bell and make a donation to enter; hours: M–Sa 10AM–12PM, 4:30PM–6PM, Su 4:30PM–6PM)*, with its charming fountain and romantic arcades.

Arts & Entertainment:

The collection at the **Museum of Musical Instruments (7)** *(P.za Santa Croce in Gerusalemme 9A, 06-701.47.96; hours: Tu–Su 8:30AM–7:30PM)* covers typically Italian pieces as well as wind, string, and percussion instruments from around the world and of all eras. The famous Barberini harp is part of the collection, as is one of the first pianos ever built, made in the  early 18th century by the instrument's inventor, Bartolomeo Cristoforo. Considerably less charming is the **Historic Museum of the Liberation of Rome (8)** *(Via Tasso 145, 06-700.38.66; hours: Tu, Th, F 4PM–7PM, Sa–Su 9:30AM–12:30PM)*, in a building that was the Gestapo's headquarters and prison during World War II. The museum honors, among others, the many antifascists who were interrogated, tortured, and jailed there.

PLACES TO EAT & DRINK
Where to Eat:

At **La Tana dei Golosi (9) (€€)** *(Via di San Giovanni in Laterano 220, 06-77.20.32.02, www.latanadeigolosi.it;*

hours: M–Sa 7PM–12AM) the menu changes twice a month: the focus on cuisine of different Italian regions has given the restaurant a faithful following of curious gourmets who delight in tasting the seasonal specialties. Organic produce, high quality ingredients, and regional wines make this a restaurant not to be missed. **Isidoro (10) (€)** *(Via San Giovanni in Laterano 59a, 06-700.82.66; call for hours)*, a great pasta bar, mostly vegetarian, offers tastings of different pasta dishes at once. Near Porta Maggiore, **Hosteria degli Artisti (11) (€€)** *(Via G. Sommeiller 6, 06-701.81.48; call for hours)* serves food from the Campania region, with an emphasis on fish and seafood.

WHERE TO SHOP

The father-son Ranati team at **Dierre Bijoux (12)** *(Via Merulana 165, 06-70.49.46.95)* makes great costume jewelry for fashion shows, movie stars, and the Miss Italia pageant. The Ranatis sell ready-made or custom-created paste. **Soul Food (13)** *(Via di San Giovanni in Laterano 192, 06-70.45.20.25, www.haterecords.com/html/soulFood.html)* stocks rare LPs and single records, both Italian and

imported; it's not cheap but vinyl freaks will have fun fishing for treasures. The flea market in **Via Sannio (14)** *(mornings, M–F; open till 6PM on Sat.)* has great buys in vintage, secondhand, and new clothes, with end-of-week sales. As with all flea markets, you need patience, but the payoff can be big if you find a fabulous bargain. And it's not as chaotic as **Porta Portese** *(see page 173)*.

CELIO

B: 60, 75, 81, 175, 271, 673; San Clemente—
85, 87, 117, 186, 571, 810, 850;
Santo Stefano Rotondo—81, 117, 673

M: B to Colosseo or Circo Massimo

• SNAPSHOT •

Tiers of historical eras, all critical to the development of Rome, are everywhere in evidence in the Celian Hill area. The foundations of the Temple of Claudius give a taste of what lies in the nearby Roman Forum. In the Celio *quartiere*, older Roman ruins gave way to early Christian edifices. Many of these, in turn, were reconstructed in medieval times, then again in the Baroque period. Over the centuries, pillaging hordes—Goths, Vandals, Saracens, Normans, among others—slashed and burned Rome, and older civilizations gave way to newer ones. But the old ones weren't swept away; they simply formed the foundations of each succeeding era. Beautiful and oppressive, wondrous and gruesome, Rome never lets go of its past.

The Celian Hill is part of the Archaeological Zone and, as such, is serene and verdant. As you stroll through the green spaces and parks of the quarter, you'll forget the violence that gave Rome its power, but you'll never shake the sense of history, art, and architecture that gave the *Caput Mundi* its genius.

PLACES TO SEE
Landmarks:

The church of **San Clemente (15)** *(Via di San Giovanni in Laterano, 06-774.00.21, www.basilicasanclemente. com; hours: M–Sa 9AM–12:30PM, 3PM–6PM, Su 10AM–12:30PM, 3PM–6PM)*

is an extraordinary example of the visible layers of history that have piled upon Rome, with a 12th-century church built on a 4th-century church, built on an ancient 2nd-century BC temple. The 12th-century medieval church is notable for its mosaics, frescoes, and dazzling examples of Cosmati work. In the lower level of the church lies the tomb of Pope Clement I, for whom the church is named.

Walking westward, you'll arrive at the green expanse of the Celio park and hill, dotted by ruins and bits of old walls and gateways, such as the **Arch of Dolabella** *(Via di San Paolo della Croce)*. A large portion of the green park was once the **Temple of Claudius**, built by Agrippina (Nero's mother) for her husband, Emperor Claudius, after she poisoned him. Some of the temple's ruins make up the foundation of the bell tower *(campanile)* of the church of **Santi Giovanni e Paolo (16)** *(P.za Santi*

Giovanni e Paolo 13, Church: 06-700.57.45, Excavations: 06-70.45.45.44, www.caseromane.it; hours: Church daily 8:30AM–12PM, 3:30PM–6PM, Excavations Th–M 10AM–1PM, 3pm–6PM). The church itself was built in the 4th century and dedicated to John and Paul, two of Constantine's Roman officers who converted to Christianity.

More interesting yet are the excavations beneath **Santi Giovanni e Paolo (16)**. To the left of the church is **Clivio di Scauro (17)**, a picturesque 2nd-century BC street built by Roman magistrate Scauro. The street passes beneath the buttresses of the church where you'll find the entrance to the excavations of ancient Roman houses. A fascinating maze of 20 rooms from four 1st-century AD buildings on various levels reveals spaces that were apparently used secretly for Christian worship in a time when that could cost you your head. Frescoes and traces of paintings also make this a worthwhile visit.

At the end of **Clivio di Scauro (17)** is an area dominated by **San Gregorio Magno (18)** *(P.za di San Gregorio Magno 1, 06-700.82.27; hours: daily 8:30AM–1PM, 3:30PM–7PM)*, a 6th-century monastery converted by Pope Gregory I (St. Gregory the Great) from what used to be his home.

Much of the Celio is composed of **Villa Celimontana (19)** *(Via della Navicella, see also page 105)* and its park, belonging to the Dukes of Mattei from 1553 to 1928.

The family villa is now the domain of the Italian Geographic Society and closed to the public. The formal gardens, however, are a beautiful public park dotted with various marble pieces from the Mattei collection. On the eastern edge of the park is **Santa Maria in Domnica (20)** *(P.za della Navicella 10, 06-700.15.19; hours: daily 9AM–12PM, 4:30PM–7PM)*, known colloquially as the *Navicella*, or "little boat," after the stone galley that stands outside it, which was most likely a temple offering made by a grateful Roman.

Across Via della Navicella and nearly opposite **Santa Maria in Domnica (20)** is Rome's oldest circular church, **Santo Stefano Rotondo (21)** *(Via di Santo Stefano Rotondo 7, 06-421.191; hours: Apr–Sept Tu–Su 9AM–12PM, 4PM–6PM, Oct–Mar Tu–Su 9:30AM–12:30PM, 3:30PM–5:30PM)*. Built in the 5th century, its Byzantine atmosphere of simplicity and spiritual contemplation is appealing, although the 16th-century frescoes are terrifying: images of martyrs being boiled in oil, flayed, torturously stretched, and having their hands chopped off are quite graphic.

Arts & Entertainment:

In June and July the **Alexanderplatz Jazz Festival** is held in the **Villa Celimontana (19)** *(see also page 104)* park, with evening concerts featuring major jazz musicians. An international crowd and jazz cognoscenti flock to hear the likes of Keith Jarrett, Lou Reed, and Roberto Gatto, among others.

The place to spot fresh talent is **Galleria Arte e Pensieri (22)** *(Via Ostilia 3a, 06-700.24.04; hours: Th–Sa 4PM–8PM)*, an art collective, which, besides showing four exhibitions annually, is a meeting place for up-and-coming and less-established artists. This is the place to check out when looking for the newest in contemporary art. The **Antiquarium Comunale (23)** *(Viale del Parco del Celio 22, 06-700.15.69; hours: Summer Tu–Sa 9AM–7PM, Su 9AM–1:30PM, Winter Tu–Sa 9AM–5PM, Su 9AM–1:30PM)* houses a collection of ancient tools and utensils used in the home as well as other artifacts. Check out **Galleria SALES (25)** *(Via dei Querceti 4-5, 06-77.59.11.22; hours: Tu–Sa 3:30PM–7:30PM, closed Aug)* for some of the best Italian, American, and British artists.

PLACES TO EAT & DRINK
Where to Eat:

In a street with remarkable hotels, **Crab (24) (€€€-€€€€)** *(Via Capo d'Africa 2, 06-77.20.36.36; hours: M 7:45PM–11:30PM, Tu–Sa 1PM–3:30PM, 8PM–11:30PM, closed Aug)* is an exceptional seafood restaurant; it's said

to have the best oysters in the city, and a fashionable crowd fills the tables of this chic venue, which architect Terry Vaina remodeled out of an old warehouse. Much less expensive is **Le Naumachie (26) (€)** *(Via Celimontana 7, 06-700.27.64; hours: daily 12PM–12AM)*, where you can enjoy traditional Roman cuisine in the brick-walled dining room or outside with a view of ancient Rome.

Bars & Nightlife:

Centrum (27) *(Hotel Capo d'Africa, Via Capo d'Africa 54, 06-77.28.01, www.hotelcapodafrica.com; call for hours)* is a hip, sleek bar in a hotel overlooking the Celio and the Colosseum. Though its specialties are whiskies and cigars, don't miss the cocktails of the *quartiere*, Caput Mundi and Colosseo. In an increasingly smart neighborhood, **Café Café (28)** *(Via dei Santi Quattro Coronati 44, 06-700.87.43; hours: mid-Mar–Sept*  *daily 11AM–1AM, Oct–mid-Mar Th–Tu 11AM–1AM)* is a perfect place for a coffee, afternoon tea, late-night drinks, or an intimate *incontro*. It boasts a hearty wine list and sixty varieties of tea, and also offers soups, salads, and cheeses. The bar **Coming Out (29)** *(Via San Giovanni in Laterano 8, 06-700.98.71, www.comingout.it; call for hours)* is a gay hotspot with a fabulous view of the Colosseum. In warmer weather, the street in front fills up with a friendly crowd.

WHERE TO SHOP

Libreria Archeologica (31) *(Via San Giovanni in Laterano 46, 06-77.25.44.41, www.archeologica.com; hours: M–Sa 10AM–7PM)* is a storehouse of books on ancient Greek and Roman art and archaeology. Wonderful maps are also part of the stock. Nearby **Arte Colosseo (32)** *(Via San Giovanni in Laterano 58, 06-709.64.04, www.artecolosseo.it)* specializes in contemporary Italian paintings, original prints (some dating from the 17th century), and antique jewelry and watches. The bookstore **Gutenberg al Colosseo (33)** *(Via San Giovanni in Laterano 112, 06-77.20.88.31, www.libriantichi.com/gutenbergalcolosseo)* focuses on classics and rare books going back as far as the 17th century. It also sells small framed prints of Rome through past centuries.

WHERE TO STAY

Hotel Capo d'Africa (34) (€€€) *(Via Capo d'Africa 54, 06-77.28.01, www.hotelcapodafrica.*

com) is a stunning, high-design hotel studded with original art by contemporary Italian artists, such as Mariano Rossano and Paolo Canevari. The penthouse terrace, where breakfast is served, has a breathtaking view of the Celian Hill, the Colosseum, and the surrounding parks. Friendly and understatedly elegant, **Hotel Lancelot (35)** (€€) *(Via Capo d'Africa 47, 06-70.45.06.15, www.lancelothotel.com)* is full of niches for quiet conversations or contemplative moments. The minimalist rooms and the lovely patio under an arbor of vines afford serenity in an area that has become abuzz with nightlife. Rooms at **Hotel dei Gladiatori (36)** (€€) *(Via Labicana 125, 06-77.59.13.80, www.hotelgladiatori.it)* have views of the ruins; suites look out onto the Colosseum. The interior design is appropriate for the quarter, with classical imitations and mosaics. The terrace at sunset is fabulous.

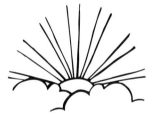

CARACALLA

• SNAPSHOT •

The central focus of the vast green area south of the Celio is the 3rd-century *Terme di Caracalla* (Baths of Caracalla). The largest public bath and entertainment center until Diocletian built his baths, the *Terme di Caracalla* is now an impressive set of ruins, with arches, doorways, and platforms that conjure images of a time when Romans rubbed elbows in waters warmed by the sun-baked marble. Keeping fit was important to the ancients: bathing and exercise attended to physical well-being while libraries and areas for meetings and discussions kept the mind fit. Today, visitors to Rome can stay fit by strolling through the Caracalla complex or walking the road that marks the beginning of the ancient Appian Way. The Caracalla area is dotted with numerous medieval churches, but the other splendid feature of the quarter is the Aurelian Wall, a very large section of which is standing and in good condition.

You must pay a fee to enter the Baths of Caracalla. Combination tickets with other site locations are available. You can visit the baths, as well as the Colosseum and the Palatine, for a fixed price. Visit or call for tickets: *Via di San Gregorio 30* and near the Arch of Titus on *Via Sacra (Roman Forum), 06-39.96.77.00.*

PLACES TO SEE
Landmarks:

While the **Baths of Caracalla (43)** and the **Aurelian Wall** are the most majestic of the landmarks in Caracalla, a number of medieval churches mark the area's verdant landscape. Frescoes, mosaics, bell towers, and other features distinguish the churches of **Santa Balbina (37)** *(P.za di Santa Balbina 8, 06-578.02.07; hours: daily 8:30AM–11:30AM),* **Santi Nereo e Achilleo (38)** *(Via delle Terme di Caracalla 28, 06-575.79.96; hours: after Easter–Oct W–M 10AM–12PM, 4PM–6PM),* **San Sisto Vecchio (39)** *(Piazzale Numa Pompilio 8, 06-77.20.51.74; hours: daily 9AM–11AM),* **San Cesareo (40)** *(Via di Porta San Sebastiano, 06-58.23.01.40; hours: Su 9AM–12:15PM, & by appt),* **San Giovanni a Porta Latina (41)** *(Via di San Giovanni a Porta Latina, 06-70.49.17.77; hours: daily 8AM–12:30PM, 3PM–6:30PM),* and **San Giovanni in Oleo (42)** *(Via di Porta Latina; ask at San Giovanni a Porta Latina).* The latter (St. John in Oil) marks the spot where St. John the Evangelist was said to have been immersed in boiling oil, but emerged from the cauldron unharmed.

The ★**BATHS OF CARACALLA (43)** *(Viale delle Terme di Caracalla 52, 06-39.96.77.00/06-575.86.26; hours: M 9AM–2PM, Tu–Su 9AM–sunset, last entry 1 hr before closing)* were built in the early 3rd century and used for more than three centuries. The *Terme* accommodated 1,600 people in the baths and gyms at any time. The gyms were more "stretch-ariums" than workout rooms for gladiators, but they served the dual purpose of keeping people physically agile and providing meeting grounds for socializing. The bathing routine followed a specified order: after the changing rooms, it was first the *laconicum* (sauna), then a series of variously heated rooms, from *caldarium* (hot) to *tepidarium* (lukewarm) to *frigidarium* (you get the idea), and finally the *natatio*, the open-air swimming pool. Greek and Latin libraries, conference rooms, art galleries, and gardens rounded out the possibilities. Beneath this enormous complex was a network of rooms and tunnels where slaves maintained the workings of the baths. They ran on treadmill wheels that pumped water to the baths and stoked the fires of ovens that heated rooms through pipes in the walls and floors. When the Goths sacked Rome in 537, they destroyed the aqueducts supplying water, and the baths fell into disrepair. Until recently, operas were held in the open air at the Baths of Caracalla (*Aida* was famously staged with live camels and horses) but archaeologists have deemed the performances too stressful to the ancient structure.

The area is also noted for tombs and columbaria, or communal tombs. The columbaria were usually built by wealthy Romans to bury the ashes of their slaves and freedmen. In the southeastern part of Caracalla are the **Columbarium of Pomponius Hylas (44)** *(Via di Porta Latina 10; special permit needed to visit this site: contact 06-67.10.38.19 for details)*, with their rows of niches. These were sold to people not wealthy enough to build their own tombs. The **Scipio Tomb (45)** *(Via di Porta San Sebastiano 9, 06-67.10.38.19, by appointment)* contains copies of the sarcophagi (stone coffins), statues, and terra cotta funerary urns of a family of generals. The originals are in the Vatican Museums.

The **Via di Porta San Sebastiano** is the upper part of the old Appian Way. It leads to the **Aurelian Wall** and the **Porta San Sebastiano (46)** *(Via di Porta San Sebastiano 18)*. The wall and its gateways, impressive feats of ancient civil engineering, were created by Emperor Aurelian in the 3rd century to protect the city when Rome began to expand beyond the then existing walls. **Porta San Sebastiano (46)** is the spectacular gateway of the **Aurelian Wall**. Tall marble blocks form the foundation for the tall battlements. You can go up the towers, which house the **Wall Museum (47)** *(see page 114)*, and walk along the walls; the view is superb. In front of the gateway is the **Arch of Drusus (48)** *(Via di Porta San Sebastiano)*, which once supported the aqueduct channeling water to the Baths of Caracalla. While the entire **Aurelian Wall** is remarkable, the section between Porta San Sebastiano and Porta Latina is especially magnificent.

Arts & Entertainment:

The **Wall Museum (47)** *(Porta San Sebastiano, Via di Porta San Sebastiano 18, 06-70.47.52.84; hours: Tu–Su 9AM–2PM)* is dedicated to the history of Rome's containment walls, with prints and models as illustrations. If you have a desire to learn about the art of gladiator fighting and how to wield a sword, you can take lessons at the nearby **Gruppo Storico Romano (49)** *(Via Appia Antica 18, 06-51.60.79.51, www.gsr-roma.com)*.

Because Caracalla is an area dedicated to ancient and medieval sites, for restaurants, bars, shops, and hotels try the Lateran or Celio *(see pages 97 and 102)* or the Aventine *(see page 143)*.

OUTSKIRTS OFF CARACALLA

Take a Bus Back Through Time

The Archeobus *(06-46.95.23.43/800-281.281, www.trambusopen.com)* leaves every hour from Termini Station and goes to the Baths of Caracalla, then takes **Via Appia Antica** to the catacombs and most of the sites listed below. You can get on and off at will. There are several stops worth checking out.

Appian Way (50)

(Via Appia Antica)

Catacombs of San Callisto (51)

(Via Appia Antica 126, 06-513.01.51, www.catacombe.roma.it; hours: Th–Tu 9AM–12PM, 2PM–5PM, closed Feb)

Catacombs of San Sebastiano (52)

(Via Appia Antica 136, 06-785.03.50, www.catacombe.org; hours: M–Sa 9AM–12PM, 2PM–5PM)

Fosse Ardeatine (53)

(Via Ardeatina 174, 06-513.67.42; hours: daily 8:15AM–5PM)

Catacombs of Domitilla (54)

(Via delle Sette Chiese 282, 06-511.03.42; hours: W–M 9AM–12PM, 2PM–5:30PM)

Tomb of Cecilia Metella (55)

(Via Appia Antica 161, 06-39.96.77.00, www.pierreci.it; hours: Tu–Su 9AM–1 hr before sunset)

chapter 5

CAPITOLINE/CAMPIDOGLIO

FORUM & COLOSSEUM

PALATINE

CAPITOLINE/CAMPIDOGLIO FORUM & COLOSSEUM PALATINE

Places to See:

1. Palazzo Venezia
2. San Marco
3. Il Vittoriano
4. Santa Maria in Aracoeli
5. Aracoeli Stairway
6. Cordonata
7. Piazza del Campidoglio
8. Palazzo Senatorio
9. CAPITOLINE MUSEUMS ★
10. Temple of Jupiter
11. Tarpeian Rock
12. Museum of Palazzo Venezia
14. Trajan's Column
15. Trajan's Markets
16. Forum of Julius Caesar
17. Mamertine Prison
18. Forum of Augustus
19. Forum of Nerva
20. Arch of Septimius Severus
21. Curia
22. Temple of Saturn
23. Rostra
24. Basilica Julia
25. Temple of Castor and Pollux
26. Arch of Titus
27. Temple of Antonius and Faustina
28. Temple of Romulus
29. Basilica of Constantine and Maxentius
30. Temple of Vesta
31. House of the Vestal Virgins
32. Antiquarium Forense
33. Santa Francesca Romana
34. Arch of Constantine
35. COLOSSEUM ★
39. Farnese Gardens
40. Cryptoporticus
41. House of Livia
42. Temple of Cybele
43. Huts of Romulus
44. Domus Flavia
45. Domus Augustana
46. Stadium
47. Domus Septimius Severus
48. Palatine Museum

Places to Eat & Drink:

13. Caffè Capitolino
36. Ristorante Mario's

Where to Stay:

37. Fori Imperiali Cavalieri
38. Forum

★ *Top Picks*

The Capitoline, the Forum, and the Palatine are areas of concentrated archaeological and historical sites. Therefore, most restaurants in these areas are tourist traps or fast food joints. Some exceptions are noted. Otherwise, it's advisable to dine in districts nearby. For restaurants, bars, shops, and hotels near the Capitoline, turn to areas such as the Pantheon or Ghetto *(see pages 40 and 46)*, the Quirinale or Monti *(see pages 77 and 84)*, or the Aventine *(see page 143)*.

CAPITOLINE/CAMPIDOGLIO

*B: 30, 40, 44, 46, 60, 62, 63, 64, 70, 81, 85, 87, 95,
117, 170, 492, 571, 628, 630, 780, 810, 850*

• SNAPSHOT •

Of Rome's seven hills, the Capitoline (*Campidoglio* or
Capitolino), though the shortest, is the most venerated.
The heart of spiritual and political activity since the
6th century BC, it was once the site of the ancient
Temple of Jupiter. It continues to be the locus of Rome's
municipal administration, with city hall housed in the
Palazzo Senatorio on the central square of Piazza del
Campidoglio.

The Capitoline is noted for its religious, political, and
historical sites. The Palazzo Senatorio, seat of the
Roman Senate from the 12th century, sits at the hill's
summit—at the Piazza del Campidoglio. The Capitol in
Washington, DC, where the U.S. Congress sits, was
named after this revered area. Symbolically, the
Capitoline represents one of the pillars of Western civilization. The imposing Piazza del Campidoglio and the
Senatorial Palace, both designed by Michelangelo, are
examples of Renaissance principles of beauty, harmony,
and symmetry, and are worth the climb. Walking
through the Capitoline is like taking a stroll through
Imperial and Renaissance Rome. The area should also be
visited at night when the lighting throws magical auras
onto the piazza and the surrounding buildings.

PLACES TO SEE
Landmarks:

At the northern foot of Capitoline Hill is **Piazza Venezia**, a large square with what seems like a perpetual traffic jam. On the west side, **Palazzo Venezia (1)** *(Via del Plebiscito 118, 06-69.99.42.84; hours: Tu–Su 8:30AM–7:30PM)*, built in the 15th century by the Venetian Pope Paul II, is one of Rome's first Renaissance buildings. Over the centuries it metamorphosed from papal residence to Venetian Embassy to French property, until ownership finally reverted to the Italian state in 1916. Mussolini made it his center of operations and stood on the central balcony to give his pompous orations. In a show of fascist insecurity, police kept the crowds moving—maybe a godsend for the many who weren't interested in standing still for *Il Duce's* speeches.

Next to **Palazzo Venezia (1)**, in a small square off **Piazza Venezia**, is the church of **San Marco (2)** *(P.za San Marco 48, 06-679.52.05; hours: M 4PM–7PM, Tu–Su 8:30AM–12:30PM, 4PM–7PM)*, founded in 336 by Pope Mark. It was built on the grounds of what legend claims was the house of St. Mark the Evangelist (patron saint of Venice). It was rebuilt in the 5th century and renovated in the 15th century by Venetian Pope Paul II when he had **Palazzo Venezia (1)** built. Its present Baroque style came from an 18th-century reconstruction. There are lions everywhere, from the medieval sculptures at the main entrance to the ceiling decorations. They were the symbol of St. Mark and the Barbo family crest of Pope Paul II. The church houses tombs of various Venetians, but the most notorious gravestone is that of Vanozza Catanei, mother of the infamous Cesare and Lucrezia Borgia, and mistress of Pope Alexander VI (Rodrigo Borgia).

Across from **San Marco (2)**, on the other side of **Piazza Venezia**, is the Victor Emmanuel Monument **Il Vittoriano (3)** *(P.za Venezia, 06-699.17.18; hours: daily 9:30AM–4PM)*, a colossal gaudy tribute to Vittorio Emanuele II, the first king of unified Italy. It has been nicknamed "the wedding cake" and "the typewriter" because of its tiers of stark marble slabs and toothlike columns in semicircular formation. A gilt bronze statue of the king astride a horse stands in the middle, atop sculpted marble. The bombastic architecture has led Romans to say that it's the perfect viewing spot in Rome—because it's the only place where you don't see **Il Vittoriano (3)**.

Behind **Il Vittoriano (3)** is the medieval church **Santa Maria in Aracoeli (4)** *(P.za d'Aracoeli, 06-679.81.55; hours: Apr–Oct daily 9AM–12:30PM, 3PM–6:30PM, Nov–Mar daily 9:30AM–12:30PM, 2:30PM–5:30PM)*. To reach this 6th-century church of "St. Mary of the Altar in the Sky," you must climb the 14th-century **Aracoeli Stairway (5)**. Some believe it was built in gratitude for the lifting of the plague of the Black Death; with 124 marble steps it might send some to their death of fatigue, the more fit to a euphoric state. When 17th-century backpacking tourists unrolled their sleeping bags on the steps, Prince Caffarelli, a hilltop inhabitant, chased them away by rolling barrels filled with stones down the steps. **Santa Maria in Aracoeli (4)** was built on the site of an ancient temple to Juno and contains works and relics spanning the 3rd century BC to the 15th century AD. The interior of the church is imposing, with 22 columns taken from ancient Roman buildings marking the central nave. A Cosmatesque floor and works (some signed) by major artists of the 13th, 14th, and 15th centuries grace the church. Relics of St. Helena, mother of 4th-century Emperor Constantine, are also located here.

Go back down the **Aracoeli Stairway (5)** (note the **Roman Insula**, ruins of a tenement building of Imperial Rome, at the foot of the stairway on the Via del Teatro di

Marcello) and up the adjoining **Cordonata (6)** *(from Via del Teatro di Marcello)*. This magnificent sweeping staircase leads up to the fabulous **Piazza del Campidoglio (7)**. Take time to relish Michelangelo's gorgeous geometrical designs on the pavement of the piazza and the graceful beauty of the surrounding buildings. In the center of the piazza is a copy of a majestic statue of Marcus Aurelius on a horse (the original is in the Palazzo Nuovo).

Facing the **Cordonata (6)** is the **Palazzo Senatorio (8)**, now the offices of the mayor of Rome.

The two other stunning buildings of the **Piazza del Campidoglio (7)** are the **Capitoline Museums (9)** *(see below)*, **Palazzo Nuovo** and **Palazzo dei Conservatori**, with collections of some of the finest specimens of art from ancient Rome up through the Renaissance and Baroque eras. Michelangelo designed the **Cordonata (6)**, the **Piazza del Campidoglio (7)**, and the façades of its palazzi (**Senatorio (8)**, **Nuovo**, and **Conservatori**), though all were completed long after his death. The **Tabularium** joins the two Capitoline Museums. It was the ancient Roman archive, the building on which the **Palazzo Senatorio (8)**, was built. Dating from 78 BC, the **Tabularium** affords a spectacular view over the Roman Forum, especially resplendent at sunset.

The **Temple of Jupiter (10)** *(Via del Tempio di Giove)*, built around 509 BC, stood at the southern apex of Capitoline Hill. Today, only ruins remain of the Grecian-style rectangular temple and its Roman podium; from those ruins archaeologists surmise the structure to have been about as big as the Pantheon. At the southern end of the temple ruins is the **Tarpeian Rock (11)** *(Via del Tempio di Giove and Via di Monte Caprino)*, *Rupe Tarpea*, the cliff from which traitors to ancient Rome were flung to their death.

Arts & Entertainment:
The ★**CAPITOLINE MUSEUMS (9)** *(P.za del Campidoglio 1, 06-82.05.91.27/06-67.10. 24.75, info 06-06.08, www.museicapitolini. org; hours: Tu–Su 9AM–8PM)* **Palazzo Nuovo** and **Palazzo**

TOP PICK!

123

dei Conservatori house bronze sculptures from the 5th century BC through the 4th century AD, Classical sculptures, and paintings by Renaissance and Baroque masters. The collection was started in 1471 when Pope Sixtus IV gave several bronze sculptures to the city. In 1566 Pope Pius V added to the holdings. By 1734 the accumulation was significant, and Pope Clement XII turned the **Palazzo Nuovo** into the first public museum in the world.

Gathered in the **Palazzo Nuovo** is one of Europe's most important collections of ancient sculpture. Many of these pieces took inspiration from or were direct copies of Greek statues. Among its many masterpieces, the museum houses the 2nd-century bronze statue of Marcus Aurelius which once stood in the center of **Piazza del Campidoglio (7)** (a copy has taken its place there); statues of drunken old men and women; the *Red Faun* (a marble satyr and the basis for Nathaniel Hawthorne's novel *The Marble Faun*); busts of emperors, philosophers, and poets; the *Dying Gaul*; and the flirtatious 1st-century BC *Capitoline Venus*. The latter was based on the Greek *Cnidian Aphrodite*, a marble figure on the island of Kos so erotic that a 4th-century BC local who embraced the goddess was caught literally with his pants down.

Once the city tribunal during the Middle Ages, the **Palazzo dei Conservatori** contains a collection of sculpture ranging from 1st-century BC bronze statues to Renaissance and Baroque marble sculptures. The famous *Spinario*, a 1st-century BC bronze of a boy taking out a splinter from his foot, is there. Also in the collection is the renowned 5th-century BC Etruscan bronze of the She-Wolf suckling Romulus and Remus (the twin babies, founders of Rome, were added in the 15th century). In the museum's courtyard is the marble head and other fragments of a huge 4th-century statue of Emperor Constantine I, taken from the Basilica of Maxentius in the Roman Forum *(see page 131)*. The museum also houses paintings by great masters such as Veronese, Tintoretto, Rubens, Caravaggio, and Titian, among others.

The **Museum of Palazzo Venezia (12)** *(see page 120)* houses a fine collection of paintings from the Renaissance through the 18th century, tapestries from around Europe, bronzes, silver, majolica, Neapolitan figurines in ceramic, and Baroque sculptures in terra cotta. In the eastern wing of the palazzo, where special exhibitions are held, you can see Mussolini's office, the *Sala del Mappamondo*, named for the 16th-century map of the world that hung there.

PLACES TO EAT & DRINK
Where to Eat:
Caffè Capitolino (13) (€) *(P.za Caffarelli 4, 06-69.19.05.64; hours: Tu–Su 9AM–8PM)* is a café on the terrace of Palazzo Caffarelli, with a spectacular view of Rome. It offers finger sandwiches, pastries, ice cream, and beverages, and is a great place to rest after all the hill climbing. The café isn't marked, so from the top of the Cordonata stairway, turn right and follow the incline.

FORUM & COLOSSEUM

B: 81, 85, 87, 117, 175, 186, 810, 850
M: B to Colosseo

• SNAPSHOT •

Adjacent to the Campidoglio is the *Foro Romano*, the ★**ROMAN FORUM.** It is on these stones that ancient republicans, emperors, philosophers, patricians, and plebeians met to discuss and debate the political, social, and judicial matters of the day. At the far eastern end of the Forum, Emperor Vespasian built the Colosseum. The stadium is amazingly well preserved, but an eeriness pervades the arena and its underground animal cages, reminding the spectator of its gory past.

Like a mass of jigsaw puzzle pieces, the Forum is a conglomeration of ruins, majestic columns, partitions, and walls, with the towering Colosseum rising in the background. All these vestiges of an ancient civilization spark

the imagination, allowing history and dreams to commingle. Here, in the Forum, was the heartbeat of the people of the Republic. Today, on that same soil in 21st-century Rome, modern humanity encounters ancient ghosts. It is an encounter you won't want to miss.

Entrances and tickets:

Via dei Fori Imperiali, Largo Romolo e Remo, Via del Foro Romano, and by the Arch of Titus (on Via Sacra), 06-39.96.77.00/06-700.54.69; hours: daily 9AM–1 hour before sunset, unless otherwise specified.

Entrance to the Roman Forum and the *Imperial Fora* is free. You must pay a fee to enter the Colosseum. Combination tickets with other site locations are available. Visit or call for tickets: *Via di San Gregorio 30* and near the Arch of Titus on *Via Sacra (Roman Forum), 06-39.96.77.00.*

The Visitors' Center provides guided tours: *Via dei Fori Imperiali, 06-679.77.86 or 06-679.77.02; hours: Apr–Sept daily 8:30AM–6:30PM, Oct–Mar daily 8:30AM–4:30PM.*

Mobile refreshment carts offer drinks and snacks. For restaurants, bars, and shops, go to the nearby Monti area *(see Chapter 3, page 84)* or the Celio *(see Chapter 4, page 102)*. Cafés and restaurants abound on nearby Via Cavour.

PLACES TO SEE
Landmarks:

In constructing Via dei Fori Imperiali, Mussolini bulldozed through ancient ruins and medieval and Renaissance buildings constructed on top of them. The street was made to connect his headquarters in Palazzo Venezia to the Colosseum. The avenue more or less separates the area of the *fora* into the **Roman Forum** to the south and the **Imperial Fora**, with some exceptions, to the north.

In the northern sector, individual emperors built administrative centers that doubled as monuments to themselves. The remains of the last of these, the 2nd-century **Forum of Trajan**, cover the northeastern part of this area. At what would have been the north end of the forum is **Trajan's Column (14)** *(Via dei Fori Imperiali)*, wonderfully sculpted and incredibly well preserved.

East of the column are **Trajan's Markets (15)** *(Via IV Novembre 94, 06-679.00.48/06-679.77.02; hours: Tu–Su 9AM–2PM)*, an early 2nd-century

shopping mall. Shops sold silks, jewelry, spices, flowers, fruit, and fish, among other products, and offices in the building rationed free corn to hungry citizens.

On the other side of Via dei Fori Imperiali is the first of the *Imperial Fora*—the **Forum of Julius Caesar (16)**

(Via del Carcere Tulliano, 06-39.96.77.00). Caesar claimed that he was descended from Venus, the goddess of love, and he built a temple in his forum dedicated to Venus Genetrix. In it were statues of Venus, Caesar, and Cleopatra.

Southwest of Caesar's Forum, at the foot of the Capitoline, is the **Mamertine Prison (17)** (*Clivio Argentario 1, 06-679.29.02; hours: Apr–Oct daily 9AM– 7, Nov–Mar daily 9AM–5PM*)—two underground dungeons, one beneath the other, where inmates were chained and left to die or executed in a lower cell.

Southeast of Caesar's and Trajan's *fora* is the **Forum of Augustus (18)** *(P.za del Grillo 1)*, opened in 2 BC to commemorate Augustus's victory over Caesar's assassins, Brutus and Cassius, in the Battle of Philippi (42 BC). Four Corinthian columns demarcate the area where the Temple of Mars the Avenger stood—with a statue of Mars suspiciously resembling Augustus himself. Walking through Augustus's shrine to himself, you reach the **Forum of Nerva (19)** *(P.za del Grillo 1, via Forum of Augustus)*. Much of it was bulldozed, along with Renaissance shops and bars built on top of it, when Mussolini built the Via dei Fori Imperiali.

In the western half of the **Roman Forum**, toward Capitoline Hill, the most spectacular and well-preserved structure is the **Arch of Septimius Severus (20)**, built in AD 203 for the tenth anniversary of Emperor Septimius Severus's rule.

The **Curia (21)** was the Roman Senate, a building destroyed several times by fire and rebuilt by Julius Caesar (52 BC), then Domitian (AD 94), and again by Diocletian (3rd century AD). Diocletian's **Curia** was restored in 1937 and is the structure existing today. The original 3rd-century floor remains, as do the speaker's platform and the risers where the 300 senators sat in council.

On the other side of the **Arch of Septimius Severus (20)** are the ruins of the **Temple of Saturn (22)**, a platform and eight enormous columns with part of the entablature above them. According to myth, the god Saturn presided over an era of peace and prosperity free from war, crime, slavery, and private property. The three nearby columns are what's left of the **Temple of Vespasian**. On the other side of the **Temple of Saturn (22)** are the ruins of the imperial **Rostra (23)**, the platform from which speeches were made to the citizens of Rome. The most famous was Mark Antony's oration after Julius Caesar was assassinated in 44 BC: "Friends, Romans, Countrymen, lend me your ears. . . ."

Off to the side of the **Temple of Saturn (22)** is a large area of stones, the remains of **Basilica Julia (24)**. In ancient Rome, basilicas were law courts and places where state fiscal matters were negotiated. Civil law cases were tried in **Basilica Julia (24)**, where 180 magistrates presided in four courtrooms. Lawyers paid people to come cheer them and boo their opponents. At the end of **Basilica**

Julia (24) is the **Temple of Castor and Pollux (25)**, first built in 484 BC to honor the mythical twins. They appeared during the Battle of Lake Regillus, helping the Romans vanquish the Tarquin kings, then showed themselves again in the Forum—on the spot where the temple was then built. Three beautiful Corinthian columns dating from AD 6, reconstructed numerous times after fires, remain.

The eastern half of the **Roman Forum** picks up at this point. Several notable ruins are located in this part of the **Via Sacra** ("Sacred Way"), the main street of the Forum and the route taken by triumphal and religious processions from the **Arch of Titus (26)** *(see page 132)* to Capitoline Hill. On the north side of the **Via Sacra** is perhaps the most bizarre sight of the entire area. The **Temple of Antonius and Faustina (27)**, with its ancient steps, columns, and front porch, is attached to the Baroque façade of the church of San Lorenzo in Miranda, making it appear as though the 2nd-century temple is capped by a Baroque hat, with the church caged by the old temple columns. The circular structure next door with a cupola on top is the **Temple of Romulus (28)**, dating from the 4th century and built for the son of Emperor Maxentius.

Continuing along the **Via Sacra**, you come to the substantial remains of the **Basilica of Constantine and Maxentius (29)**, the largest structure in the Forum. This 4th-century building was begun by Maxentius, emperor of the Western part of then-split Rome, and completed by Constantine. After Contantine conquered Maxentius in battle in AD 312, he became ruler of the entire Western Roman Empire. Three enormous coffered barrel vaults give a sense of the immensity of the original building.

Across the **Via Sacra** to the south, and past a middle area of ruins, are the remains of the **Temple of Vesta (30)** and of the **House of the Vestal Virgins (31)**. The Temple was dedicated to Vesta, goddess of the hearth, and her cult of the Vestals, six virgins charged with keeping the sacred flame of Vesta continuously lit. The Vestals, the only female priests in Rome, came from noble families, had to be virgins, and were granted privileges that no other women in Rome had. As soon as they were chosen for service, the girls were taken to live in the **House of the Vestal Virgins (31)** with the other priestesses. A large three-story building with around 50 rooms, the house had a central courtyard with a lily pond and goldfish. To the east of the Vestals' ruins is the **Arch of Titus (26)**, a triumphal monument built in AD 81 to commemorate Vespasian and his son Titus's sacking of Jerusalem.

Directly north of the arch is the **Antiquarium Forense (32)**, a small archaeological museum *(see page 134)*. It is housed within the church **Santa Francesca Romana (33)**, where a flagstone is marked with the supposed knee prints of Saints Peter and Paul. Just beyond the Forum to the east is the **Arch of Constantine (34)** *(between Via San Gregorio and P.za del Colosseo)*, a monument to Constantine's victory over Maxentius.

Constantine's arch stands beside one of Rome's most famous and emblematic structures, the ★**COLOSSEUM (35)** *(P.za del Colosseo, 06-700.54.69/06-39.96.77.00; hours: daily 9AM–sunset)*. When Nero committed suicide in AD 68, his outrageously opulent house **Domus Aurea** *(see page 86)*, where he held orgies and decadent garden parties, was demolished. The lake was drained, and in its place Emperor Vespasian built the **Colosseum (35)**. The majestic amphitheatre seated at least 55,000 (some say 87,000) people, who entered and exited through 80 arched entrances. Internal corridors allowed rapid access to the seating areas. This architectural plan has formed the basis for amphitheaters and sports arenas to this day.

Blood sport was the hallmark of the **Colosseum (35)**, with the combatants any combination of professionally trained gladiators (who were slaves, condemned criminals, and prisoners of war), untrained unfortunates, and wild animals fighting one another to the death. While entry to the gory shows was free, the spectators were separated by social class and sex. The central box with front-row seats was reserved for the emperor and senators; priests and magistrates had the next tier up, and above them were foreign diplomats. Women were relegated to the top floor, except for the Vestal Virgins, who had front-row seating alongside the emperor. Wild animal fights were finally abolished in AD 523.

Arts & Entertainment:

Antiquarium Forense (32), the Archaeological Museum of the Forum, located within the convent of **Santa Francesca Romana (33)**, contains pieces excavated from the Forum. Iron Age funerary urns, skeletons, and fragments of statues and architectural details from buildings in the Forum are part of the collection.

PLACES TO EAT & DRINK
Where to Eat:

Typical Roman dishes are served at the pleasant outdoor tables of **Ristorante Mario's (36)** (€–€€) *(P.za del Grillo 9, 06-679.37.25, www.ristorantemarios.com; hours: Tu–Su 12PM–3:30PM, 6:30PM–11PM)*. Nearby, in the Monti area *(see page 84)* are more restaurants.

WHERE TO STAY

A couple of hotels in the Forum area are worth considering. The **Fori Imperiali Cavalieri (37)** (€€) *(Via Frangipane 34, 06-679.62.46, www.cavalieri.it)* is quiet with excellent service and good value for the style and comfort it offers. The hotel has been renovated and includes dataports in the rooms. **Forum (38)** (€€) *(Via Tor de' Conti 25-30, 06-679.24.46, www.hotelforum rome.com)*, a converted convent, is warm and pleasant, with walnut paneling and a roof-garden restaurant with a view of the **Imperial Fora**. It does not, however, have A/C.

Also check out hotels in the nearby Monti area *(see page 89)*, the Celio *(see page 108)*, or the Aventine *(see page 149)*.

PALATINE

B: 60, 75, 85, 87, 117, 175, 271, 571, 673, 810, 850
M: B to Circo Massimo or Colosseo

• SNAPSHOT •

In ancient times, the affluent and powerful made their
homes on the hills, whose elevation and distance from
the swampy valleys in between made them desirable. Of
these, the Palatine was the most exclusive residential
location. It was close enough to the business and political center of the Forum but far enough away to be quiet
and pleasant. The first emperor, Augustus, was born
there and lived in a modest home. Emperors Tiberius,
Caligula, and Domitian built palatial homes on the hill.
Nero's *Domus Aurea*, centered on the Esquiline and
Celio Hill, encompassed an area reaching as far as the
Palatine, with his large lake in the valley between them
(in what is now the Colosseum). But well before
Imperial Rome (27 BC to AD 476), before even the
Republic (509 BC to 27 BC), Romulus
founded Rome on the Palatine in 753
BC. According to the famous legend,
the twins Romulus and Remus were
raised by a she-wolf in a cave on Palatine
Hill. Archaeologists believe that Iron
Age huts (dating from the 9th to 7th
centuries BC) on the Palatine were the
first settlements of Rome.

ENTRANCE AND TICKETS:

You must pay a fee to enter the Palatine. Combination tickets with other site locations are available. Visit or call for tickets: *Via di San Gregorio 30* and near the Arch of Titus on *Via Sacra (Roman Forum), 06-39.96.77.00/06-699.01.10. Hours: daily 9AM–sunset.*

For restaurants, bars, shops, and hotels, go to the nearby areas of the Celio *(see page 102)* or the Aventine *(see page 143)* or slightly further, to the Monti district *(see page 84).*

PLACES TO SEE
Landmarks:

From the **Roman Forum**, you can enter the Palatine at the **Farnese Gardens (39)**. It was built in the 16th century by Cardinal Alessandro Farnese on the ruins of the *Domus Tiberius* (*domus* means "house," and the houses of most of the emperors here were palaces). The wonderful 17th-century pavilion at the top of the hill has fabulous views of the Forum. Behind this pavilion, along the garden's southeastern border is the **Cryptoporticus (40)**, an underground tunnel that was part of a network connecting Nero's *Domus Aurea* in the Esquiline to Palatine Hill. Stucco reliefs ornament the vaults, and slits allow light to filter in.

One of the better-preserved buildings on the Palatine is near the southern tip of the **Farnese Gardens (39)**. The **House of Livia (41)** is where Emperor Augustus lived with Livia, his second wife. Faded frescoes give a sense of the decoration of this imperial domicile, and though it was more modest than that of later emperors, it has lasted longer. Some of the frescoes depict mythological scenes; others are *trompe-l'oeil* paintings.

Near Livia's house are the ruins of the **Temple of Cybele (42)**, a mother-figure goddess sacred to a 2nd-century BC cult. The cult's priests castrated themselves in wild ritual sacrifices to the goddess, who reigned over the fertility of nature. All that remains of the temple is

rubble, a platform, and a decapitated statue of Cybele. Nearby are the remnants of three huts dating from the 9th century BC—the **Huts of Romulus (43)**. Romulus, whom Rome was named after, killed his twin Remus and established the city here.

In AD 81 Emperor Domitian of the Flavian dynasty built a palace that was to be the imperial residence for the next 300 years. It had two sections. **Domus Flavia (44)** was the official palace while **Domus Augustana (45)** was the private home. A courtyard, fountains, and dining room were at the entrance of **Domus Flavia (44)**. The name of the **Domus Augustana (45)**, Domitian's private home, derives from the Latin *augustus*, which means "favored by the gods." Domitian may have been august, but he was also paranoid. Terrified of being murdered, he had his courtyard walls lined with shiny stones to act as mirrors in which he could spy an intruder. This didn't prevent him from being assassinated in his bedroom; one theory is that his wife was behind it.

An oblong **Stadium (46)** to the east of the **Domus Augustana (45)** was part of the palace. Its use is unknown; it may have been a racetrack or garden. In the 6th century it was used for footraces. The wall fragments and arches to the south are part of the **Domus Septimius Severus (47)**, a 2nd-century AD extension of the imperial palace.

Arts & Entertainment:

The **Palatine Museum (48)**, tucked between the **Domus Flavia (44)** and the **Domus Augustana (45)**, is an *antiquarium* of objects and pieces of buildings from the Palatine. These include artifacts and human remains from the 8th-century BC hilltop settlements, as well as models of the huts, and statues, busts, and eave decorations. Parts of the foundation of Domitian's palace are evident in the museum's structure.

chapter 6

AVENTINE
TESTACCIO
OSTIENSE

AVENTINE TESTACCIO OSTIENSE

Places to See:
1. San Teodoro
2. Santa Maria della Consolazione
3. Casa dei Crescenzi
4. Temple of Portunus
5. Temple of Hercules Victor
6. Santa Maria in Cosmedin
7. Circo Massimo
8. Roseto di Roma
9. Parco Savello
10. Santa Sabina
11. Piazza dei Cavalieri di Malta
12. Sant'Anselmo
29. Monte Testaccio
30. Protestant Cemetery
31. Pyramid of Caius Cestius
32. MACRO Future
33. Villaggio Globale
34. Teatro di Documenti
50. Centrale Montemartini
56. San Paolo Fuori Le Mura

Places to Eat & Drink:
13. Trattoria San Teodoro
14. Fienile
16. Osteria del Campidoglio
17. Alvaro al Circo Massimo
18. Clamur
35. Volpetti Più
36. Luna Piena
37. Letico
38. Augustarello
39. Checchino dal 1887
40. Joia
41. Divinare
42. Café de Oriente
43. Caffè Latino
44. Alibi
51. Alpheus
52. Ex-Magazzini
53. Sonar
54. Nazca

Where to Shop:
20. Longobardi
21. Il Negozio Benedettino della Badia Primaziale di Sant'Anselmo
45. Testaccio Market
46. Volpetti
47. Le Bambole
48. Boccanera

Where to Stay:

Rome is the city of echoes,
the city of illusions, and
the city of yearning.

—*Giotto di Bondone*

AVENTINE

B: P.za Bocca della Verità—23, 44, 63, 81,
95, 160, 170, 280, 628, 715, 716, 780, 781;
Santa Sabina—23, 280, 716

M: B to Circo Massimo or Piramide

• SNAPSHOT •

Some 2,000 years ago the area along the Tiber River in the Aventine stirred with commerce and river transportation. The ports gave the area a rough quality, and sailors and merchants took up quarters there. In the triangle between the northern foot of Aventine Hill and Capitoline Hill, in the area around what is now Piazza Bocca della Verità, the outdoor markets of Forum Boarium (cattle) and Forum Holitorium (vegetables) were frequented by plebeians.

The plebeians, the lowest class of Roman citizens, were made up of peasants, traders, builders, and other manual laborers. As the merchants on Aventine Hill became more affluent, they constructed their own homes, and the area began to undergo gentrification. By 27 BC, the beginning of the Empire, the Aventine had become upscale; by the 5th century it was dotted with luxury palazzi. Today, the Aventine is an exclusive residential neighborhood, full of expensive villas with luxurious gardens and swimming pools. Quiet, tree-lined, and relatively secluded, Aventine Hill nevertheless encompasses a number of noteworthy landmarks and one of Rome's loveliest green spots, Parco Savello.

PLACES TO SEE
Landmarks:

One of Rome's little gems is **San Teodoro (1)** *(Via di San Teodoro 7, 06-678.66.24; hours: Su–F 9:30AM–12:30PM)*, a 6th-century church snuggled into the foot of Palatine Hill in the triangle along the river formed by the Aventine, Capitoline, and Palatine. The small round exterior, built on the ruins of an ancient granary, is intriguing, while the splendid interior is marked by its 6th-century mosaics and 15th-century Florentine cupola. Not far away, beneath the cliff of the **Tarpeian Rock** *(see page 123)*, where criminals and traitors were dropped to their deaths, stands **Santa Maria della Consolazione (2)** *(P.za della Consolazione 84, 06-678.46.54; hours: daily 6:30AM–12PM, 3:30PM–6PM)*. It was named after an image of the Virgin Mary that 14th-century nobleman Giordanello degli Alberini, a condemned man himself, had placed there to console the unfortunates as they plunged over the cliff. That icon is located in the church's presbytery.

In the area along the riverfront are numerous structures, in various states of preservation, that are reminders of the busy cattle market that once energized the docks in this district. Fragments of ancient Roman buildings are still embedded in the ruins of the 11th-century **Casa dei Crescenzi (3)** *(Via Luigi Petroselli)*, a fortress built by the Crescenzi family to control the docks and collect tolls from the Ponte Rotto. For more divine protection, the two 2nd-century BC temples of the Forum Boarium are in excellent shape because they were turned into Christian churches during the Middle Ages. The **Temple of Portunus (4)** *(P.za della Boccadella Verità)*, dedicated to the god of rivers and ports but once called the Temple of *Fortuna Virilis*, or "Men's Fortunes," is a rectangular structure with columns on the front porch. Behind it is the other shrine, small and circular: the **Temple of Hercules Victor (5)** *(P.za della Boccadella Verità)*. It was dedicated to the he-man who killed a giant for stealing his cattle. Because this small circular shrine resembles the Temple of Vesta in the Roman Forum, it has also been called by that name.

The beautiful 6th-century **Santa Maria in Cosmedin (6)** *(P.za Bocca della Verità 18, 06-678.14.19; hours: Apr–Sept daily 9AM–6PM, Oct–Mar daily 9AM–5PM)* has an amusing mix of medieval and Romanesque designs, with a 12th-century bell tower and beautiful mosaics inside. The church is most famous for the large stone mask embedded in the portico wall. The face of a man with wild hair, full beard, and mouth agape, the **Bocca della Verità**, or "Mouth of Truth," is the legendary test of lying criminals and cheating spouses. A liar who put his/her hand in the mouth, the legend has it, would end up without a hand—the stone jaws would clamp down and cut it off!

Off to the southeast of the Mouth of Truth, and below the Palatine, stretches the ancient Roman chariot-racing arena, the **Circo Massimo (7)** *(Via del Circo Massimo)*, in use from the 4th century BC until AD 549. Now just a grassy expanse, the stadium once held 300,000 spectators. The Aventine is home to several beautiful parks. Southwest of the **Circo Massimo (7)**, off the Piazzale Ugo la Malfa, is the **Roseto di Roma (8)** *(Clivio dei Pubblici)*, at the foot of the hill. This park, once the 17th-century site of a Jewish cemetery, was turned into a rose garden in the 1950s with avenues placed to form the shape of a menorah.

To the west, atop Aventine Hill, **Parco Savello (9)** *(P.za Pietro d'Illiria)*, officially **Il Giardino degli Aranci,** or "Garden of the Orange Trees," is one of Rome's gems. It has a fabulous view stretching from Gianicolo Hill and St. Peter's Basilica, across the river to the **Il Vittoriano** in Piazza Venezia. Located within the walls of the Savelli family fortress, the park is full of orange trees, commemorating St. Dominic, who first brought orange trees to Italy from Spain in 1220. The original tree supposedly still thrives in the garden of **Santa Sabina (10)** *(P.za Pietro d'Illiria 1, 06-57.94.06.00/06-574.35.73; hours: daily 6:30AM–12:45PM, 3:30PM–7PM),* an early Christian basilica. Built in the 5th century on what was once the home of a martyred Roman woman named Sabina, the magnificent interior is arcaded along the nave with 24 Corinthian columns.

The beautiful walled **Piazza dei Cavalieri di Malta (11)** was designed by Piranesi in the 18th century, with cypress trees, obelisks, and military trophies adding to its ornate allure. If you see people peeping through the keyhole of the **Priory of the Knights of Malta** (at No. 3), don't be appalled—they're looking at the famous key-hole view of the dome of St. Peter's Basilica across the river in the Vatican.

Arts & Entertainment:

Free concerts and church music are common in Rome's hundreds of churches, but few have what is offered at the Aventine. On Sundays (October–July) at 8:30AM mass and 7:15PM vespers, the Benedictine church of **Sant'Anselmo (12)** *(P.za Cavalieri di Malta 5, 06-579.11, www.santanselmo.net)* echoes with Gregorian chants.

PLACES TO EAT & DRINK
Where to Eat:

Chic, inviting, and upscale, **Trattoria San Teodoro (13) (€€€)** *(Via dei Fienili 49-51, 06-678.09.33; hours: M–Sa 12:30PM–3:30PM, 7:30PM–12AM)* is known for its sophisticated cui-sine—especially the seafood. The set-ting, on a quiet medieval street, is beautiful—especially the romantic patio outside. Great for a casual lunch of *panini* and pastries, **Fienile (14) (€)** *(Via dei Fienili 49-51, 06-*

6/9.08.49; hours: M–Sa 1PM–3PM, 8PM–11PM) is also a good wine bar. Indulging in some traditional Roman people-watching from the sidewalk tables makes a sandwich of *speck* and parmesan even more delightful.

Next door at **Osteria del Campidoglio (16)** (€) *(Via dei Fienili 56, 06-678.02.50; call for hours)*, you can count on good Roman favorites, such as hot dishes like *bucatini all'amatriciana*. Tables outside have a view of **Santa Maria della Consolazione (2)**. Or, if you don't want to be reminded of unfaithful wives plunging to their death from the **Tarpeian Rock**, be comforted inside the brick-faced dining room.

The reasonable prices at **Alvaro al Circo Massimo (17)** (€) *(Via dei Cerchi 53, 06-678.61.12; hours: Tu–Sa 12:30PM–3:30PM, 7PM–11PM, Su 12:30PM–3:30PM)* make this laid-back seafood restaurant a good deal. Try the linguini with lobster sauce, risotto with truffles, or grilled porcini mushrooms.

Bars & Nightlife:

Clamur (18) *(P.za dell'Emporio 2, 06-575.45.32; hours: Su–Th 7PM–12AM, F–Sa 7PM–1:30AM)* is an English pub with an Italian flair. English ales and lagers abound. For a livelier nightlife, check out the bars and clubs in Testaccio and Ostiense *(see pages 151 and 157)*, or Monti *(see page 84)*.

WHERE TO SHOP

At **Longobardi (20)** *(Via dei Fienili 43/A, 06-678.11.04)*, the wares are silver and gold, from jewelry to tableware, all made in Italy. In a cute cottage beside the Benedictine abbey of **Sant'Anselmo (12)**, **Il Negozio Benedettino della Badia Primaziale di Sant'Anselmo (21)** *(P.za dei Cavalieri di Malta 5, 06-579.11)* sells things made in monasteries worldwide. Beer made by Trappist monks, soaps concocted in distant monasteries, jams, tomato sauces, and fruit juices are among the specialties. But its forte is the cosmetics section, with lovely creams made from natural products and miraculous potions for wrinkles, cellulite, and various ailments. Be sure to try the abbey's own chocolates.

WHERE TO STAY

Great location and fantastic views (the **Roman Forum**) are the draws at **Kolbe Hotel Rome (22)** (€€€–€€€€) *(Via di San Teodoro 44, 06-69.92.42.50/06-679.88.66, www.kolbehotel rome)*; this luxury hotel features a spectacular garden. Opposite the Temple of Hercules Victor, **Forty Seven (23)** (€€) *(Via Petroselli 47, 06-678.78.16, www.forty sevenhotel.com)* is a modern temple of repose. The stern exterior belies a light-filled interior with rooms accented by natural wood and marble bathrooms. Modern amenities include Wi-Fi Internet and a fitness center. Well-appointed suites with kitchenettes make **Residence Palazzo al Velabro (24)** (€–€€) *(Via del Velabro 16, 06-679.27.58, www.velabro.it)* like a home away from home. Quiet and serene, it's a good choice for a longer stay.

The three Aventino San Anselmo hotels *(06-57.00.57, www.aventinohotels.com)* look like Tuscan villas, with a country twist to the elegant Rococo décor. The spacious rooms are as inviting as the lovely gardens surrounded by pine groves. **Hotel Aventino (25)** (€-€€) *(Via San Domenico 10)*; **Hotel San Anselmo (26)** (€-€€) *(P.za San Anselmo 2)*; **Hotel Villa San Pio (27)** (€-€€) *(Via Santa Melania 19)*.

A transformed 14th-century convent with a 17th-century façade, **Hotel Domus Aventina (28)** (€€) *(Via di Santa Prisca 11B, 06-574.61.35, www.domus-aventina.com)* is elegant, demure, and serene. Copies of classical artifacts, prints, and murals add to the refined ambience, while the views from the terrace and balconies are beautiful.

TESTACCIO

B: Protestant Cemetery area—23, 60, 75, 118, 271, 715; Monte Testaccio area: 23, 30, 75, 280, 716

M: B to Piramide

• SNAPSHOT •

Testaccio got its name from the huge amount of terra cotta shards *(testae)* that piled up over the centuries in a "mountain" as work- ers at wine and olive oil warehouses along the river threw out broken clay jugs that stored the goods. A working- class area in the shadow of the bour-

geois luxury of the Aventine, Testaccio is one of Rome's hottest nightspots and a magnet for artists, writers, and students seeking an edgier night scene.

What has defined the district since the 19th century is the old slaughter- house, now being transformed into a cultural center. Though the slaughter- house closed in 1973, many of its workers still live in the neighborhood.

This elderly population gives the area its lively color and diversity. Where soccer teams are concerned, however, there's no diversity whatsoever; the locals are staunch supporters of AS Roma, and the team's red and yellow colors are evident all over the place.

PLACES TO SEE
Landmarks:

Monte Testaccio (29) (*Via Galvani, corner of Via N. Zabaglia 24*) isn't a hill at all; it's a 118-foot rubbish pile of broken terra cotta pots used by ancient traders and shopkeepers to transport and store goods. For some 400 years (from about 140 BC to about AD 250) the shards accumulated into an artificial hill that wasn't recognized for what it is until the late 18th century.

In 1738 the Non-Catholic Cemetery, better known as the **Protestant Cemetery (30)** (*Cimitero Acattolico, Via Caio Cestio 6, 06-574.19.00, www.protestantcemetery.it; hours: M–Sa 9AM–5PM, Su 9AM–1PM*), became the burial ground for anyone who wasn't Catholic. Glorious cypresses tower above impressive funerary sculptures, and people from around the world arrive to honor the memories of famous writers, artists, and statesmen, including Goethe, Keats, and Shelley. An afternoon spent here is a reminder of the allure of the Eternal City for which so many foreigners gave up their homelands and to which they left their remains forever. Near the cemetery to the northeast is another burial ground of a wholly monumental variety. The **Pyramid of Caius Cestius (31)** (*P.zzale Ostiense*) is a huge marble pyramid, the tomb of a wealthy and clearly egomaniacal magistrate who died in 12 BC. It was incorporated into the **Aurelian Wall** near the Porta San Paolo.

Arts & Entertainment:

The old *mattatoio*, the slaughter-house, was for nearly two centuries the defining point of Testaccio, assuring work for its residents. The area is rapidly turning into a "City

of the Arts," with plans for museums, multimedia exhibition spaces, the university's architecture department, and a music school. **MACRO Future (32)** *(P.za Orazio Giustiniani 4; hours: Tu–Su 4PM–12AM; 06-671.07. 04.00, www.macro.roma.museum)*, with its two exhibition spaces, is a branch of the **Museum for Contemporary Art of Rome (MACRO)** *(see page 20)* where exhibits of contemporary Italian artists are open until late into the night.

During the winter an old *mattatoio* is also home to the **Villaggio Globale (33)** *(Lungotevere Testaccio 2/Via di Monte Testaccio 22, 06-575.72.33, www.vglobale.biz; call for hours/shows)*, one of the oldest community centers in Rome. Live concerts, art exhibits, a gay festival, and other events take place in an atmosphere of general joviality in which people mill around with their friends, checking out the wares at commercial stalls and enjoying *panini* and beer from one of the numerous kiosks. In a wonderfully atmospheric setting, the **Teatro di Documenti (34)** *(Via Nicola Zabaglia 42, 06-574.40.34, www.teatrodidocumenti.it; hours: info/reservations M–F 10:30AM–2:30PM)* presents theater performances where the audience moves along with the actors, up and down into the various wonderful spaces of this 15th-century building.

PLACES TO EAT & DRINK
Where to Eat:

The Volpetti brothers, proprietors of the famous deli *(see page 156)*, expanded their food emporium to a cafeteria *(tavola calda)* around the corner from the store. At **Volpetti Più (35)** (€) *(Via Alessandro Volta 8, 06-574.23.52, www.volpetti.com; hours: M–Sa 10:30AM–3:30PM, 5:30PM–9:30PM, Aug M–Sa 10:30AM–3:30PM)* the décor is totally practical but the food is delicious. Lasagnas, salads, pizzas, and other fabulous prepared foods assure the place is always full of customers. At the end of the block, **Luna Piena (36)** (€-€€)*(Via Luca della Robbia 15-17, 06-575.02.79; hours: Tu–Th, call for hours)*, a neighborhood trattoria, offers traditional Italian dishes along with more adventurous creations. Friendly and casual, it is decorated with contemporary art pieces.

The popular **Letico (37)** (€€) *(Via Galvani 64, 06-57.25.05.39; call for hours)*, with its warm dark wood and modern designs, has lighter versions of the Roman standards. More traditional and working-class, **Augustarello (38)** (€) *(Via Giovanni Branca 98, 06-574.65.85; call for hours)* is a neighborhood standard serving dishes native to Testaccio: lamb and potatoes, tongue, and *rigatoni alla pajata* (pasta with veal intestines) are true to the meatpacking district's heritage. One of the area's more elegant restaurants, **Checchino dal 1887 (39)** (€€) *(Via di Monte Testaccio 30, 06-574.38.16, www.checchino-dal-1887.com; hours: Tu–Sa 12:30PM–3PM, 8PM–12AM)* has a mixed menu, including often-overlooked offal (oxtails, hooves, and heads) as well as more refined dishes, such as *agnello alla cacciatora* (lamb with chilli peppers and red wine) or *saltimbocca alla romana* (veal with ham and sage), and a great wine list.

The wine bar **Divinare (41) (€)** *(Via Aldo Manuzio 12/13, 06-57.25.04.32; M–Sa 10AM–3PM, 5PM–11PM)* offers an excellent range of cold cuts, *carpaccios*, cheeses, salads, and prepared foods with a large choice of wines.

Bars & Nightlife:

Joia (40) *(Via Galvani 20, 06-574.08.02, www.joia cafe.it; call for hours)*, a bar-club-restaurant on three floors, carries the ancient Roman theme of decadence and a 17th-century sense of style into its superhip 21st-century surroundings. Trendy **Café de Oriente (42)** *(Via di Monte Testaccio 36, 06-574.50.19, www.caruso cafedeoriente.com; hours: Tu–Su 10PM–4AM)* is the hip-shaking place for salsa dancing. **Caffè Latino (43)** *(Via di Monte Testaccio 96, 06-57.28.85.56,www.caffelatino roma.com; hours: Tu–Su 10:30PM–3AM)* is the granddaddy of the area's disco-bars, with live concerts, acid jazz, and reggae. **Alibi (44)** *(Via di Monte Testaccio 40-44, 06-574.34.48; hours: Th–Su 11:30PM–5AM)*, Rome's most well-known gay disco, also attracts a mixed crowd. It's another multilevel nightspot with a terrace from which you can check out the human river that enlivens the night.

WHERE TO SHOP

Fresh, cheap produce isn't the only thing for sale at the **Testaccio Market (45)** *(P.za di Testaccio)*; while the produce stalls are a trip, there's also appeal in the high-quality shoes at factory prices. But it's a hit-or-miss shopping experience. Since 1972, the Volpetti brothers have run their gourmet deli with meticulous regard to detail and to the purity of the regional products they sell. You could become addicted to **Volpetti (46)** *(Via Marmorata 47, 06-574.23.52, www.volpetti.com)*, where cheeses, cold cuts, and specialty products come from all parts of Italy.

Dolls, dolls, and more dolls! **Le Bambole (47)** *(Via Luca della Robbia 11, 06-575.68.95, www.lebambole-testaccio. it)* has the doll market covered, with new, period, and specialty dolls. Saints, madonnas, and Neapolitan crèche pieces are in the offering. It's also a doll hospital, with restorations done by the owner. With all the traipsing up and down hills and in and out of bars, you may feel the urge for a new pair of shoes: check out the footwear at **Boccanera (48)** *(Via Luca della Robbia 36, 06-575.68.04, www.boccanera.it)*.

WHERE TO STAY

The serene park on the grounds of **Santa Prisca (49)** (€) *(Largo M. Gelsomini 25, 06-574.19.17, www.hotelsanta prisca.it)* and its terraces make up for the dormitory feeling of this converted convent owned by nuns (but not run by them). For more hotel options, check out the Aventine area *(see page 149)*.

OSTIENSE

B: To Montemartini, 23, 716, 769
M: B to Garbatella or Basilica San Paolo

• SNAPSHOT •

Ostiense may lack the charm of Testaccio, but it's break-ing out as the trendsetter in clubs, cafés, artists' studios, and shops. People have been converting the area's old warehouses and power stations into bars and nightspots. As prices rise in other neighborhoods, Ostiense is set to welcome artists, students, and young designers. The most remarkable sight worth visiting during daytime is the Centrale Montemartini, once an electrical power plant, now a fabulous museum. Otherwise, Ostiense is unremarkable by day; rather, the protagonists make their entrance at night.

PLACES TO SEE
Landmarks, Arts & Entertainment:

As Ostiense picks up momentum in its new incarnation as the "in" nightspot, the warehouses and lofts of the dis-trict are being converted into artists' studios, bars, and clubs. The 1921 **Centrale Montemartini (50)** *(Via Ostiense 106, 06-574.80.30, www.centralemontemartini.org; hours: Tu–Su 9AM–7PM)*, Rome's first electric power plant, has been converted into a hip branch of the **Capitoline Museums**. Hellenic statues—gods, goddesses, coy nymphs, leering fauns—mingle with steel tubes, hydraulic pumps, and other machinery of the old generating station in marvelous, provocative coexistence.

PLACES TO EAT & DRINK
Bars & Nightlife:

If you've checked out the hot spots in Testaccio and are aching for more, Ostiense is the next happening area for nightlife. One of the most famous clubs is **Alpheus (51)** *(Via del Commercio 36, 06-574.78.26, www.alpheus.it; call for hours)*, with three separate areas in a converted warehouse, each featuring different music-dance genres with live concerts, cabarets, and famous DJs. Friday nights are the most wild. Another converted warehouse popular with the trendy crowd is **Ex-Magazzini (52)** *(Via dei Magazzini Generali 8 bis, 06-575.80.40; hours: Tu–Su 9PM–4AM)* *(magazzini* means "warehouses"). The entertainment is diverse: music, film, theatre, and naturally the bar. On Sundays there's even an ethnic market on the lower ground floor, with wares from India and Indonesia. **Sonar (53)** *(Via dei Conciatori 7c, 06-45.42.69.50; hours: daily 11PM–3AM)* is a club popular with students and young people. Hip-hop, R&B, funk, and afrobeat keep the place open all night. **Nazca (54)** *(Via del Gazometro 40, 06-45.44.73.72, www.nazca roma.com; hours: daily from 7PM)* is a popular stop on the club circuit.

WHERE TO STAY

Hotel Abitart (55) (€€) *(Via P. Matteucci 10-20, 06-454.31.91, www.abitarthotel.com)* is the only hotel in the Ostiense area. Its eight suites are inspired by different artists, from Picasso to Keith Haring.

San Paolo Fuori Le Mura (56)
(Via Ostiense 186, 06-541.03.41)
B: 23, 128, 170, 670, 707, 761, 769
M: B to Basilica San Paolo

In the early 4th century, Emperor Constantine set about legalizing Christianity, building churches in Rome, and spreading the new religion throughout the Empire. He created several basilicas to make the acceptance of Christianity official and to commemorate the martyrdom of important saints. Thus, he built **San Paolo Fuori le Mura** over the tomb of St. Paul, who was martyred some time after AD 62, perhaps in Nero's persecution of Christians. As a Roman citizen, St. Paul could not be crucified; rather, he was executed by decapitation at the nearby **Abbey of the Three Fountains** (named for the three fountains that supposedly gushed up on the spots where Paul's severed head bounced three times). **San Paolo Fuori le Mura** is one of the four major basilicas in Rome, along with St. Peter's, San Giovanni in Laterano, and Santa Maria Maggiore (all but the last were built by Constantine).

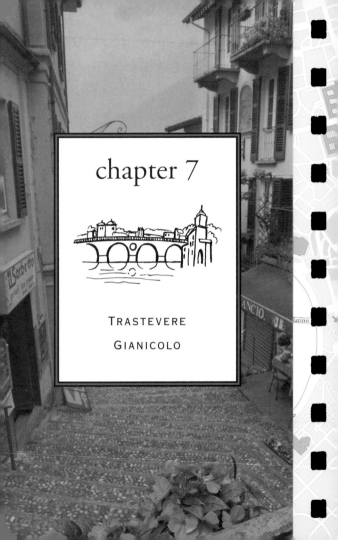

chapter 7

TRASTEVERE

GIANICOLO

TRASTEVERE
GIANICOLO

Places to See:
1. Ponte Sisto
2. Porta Settimiana
3. Casa della Fornarina
4. Museo di Roma in Trastevere
5. Santa Maria in Trastevere
6. San Crisogono
7. Caserma dei Vigili della VII Coorte
8. Piazza in Piscinula
9. Santa Cecilia in Trastevere
10. San Francesco a Ripa
11. Chiostro dei Genovesi
12. Villa Sciarra
14. Bibli
15. Big Mama
16. Lettere Caffè
17. Teatro Vascello
18. Nuovo Sacher
19. Pasquino
42. Villa Farnesina
43. Palazzo Corsini/Galleria Nazionale d'Arte Antica
44. Orto Botanico
45. Tempietto
46. Fontana dell'Acqua Paola
47. Garibaldi Monument
48. Anita Garibaldi Monument
49. Teatro Ghione
50. Filmstudio
51. Galleria Lorcan O'Neill

Places to Eat & Drink:
20. Checco er Carettiere
21. Doppia Coppia
22. Da Vittorio
23. Alberto Ciarla
24. La Scala
25. Big Hilda Café
26. Mr. Brown
27. Friends Art Café
28. Stardust
30. Bar Trilussa
53. Antico Arco
54. Bar Gianicolo
55. Antica Pesa
56. ATM Sushi Bar
60. Antico Tevere
61. RipArte Caffè
62. Il Cortile

Where to Shop:
31. Pandora della Malva
32. Officina della Carta
33. Joseph Debach
34. Scala Quattordici
35. Almost Corner Bookshop

Rome was a poem pressed
into service as a city.

—*Anatole Broyard*

TRASTEVERE

B: *Museo di Roma*—3, 8, 23, 44, 75, 116, 280, 630, 780; *Santa Maria and Santa Cecilia*—23, 280, 630, 780; *San Francesco*—23, 44, 280

• SNAPSHOT •

Trastevere (literally "across the Tiber," or *Tevere*) is a historical quarter that was once agricultural. Farms, vineyards, and gardens served the emperors. Separated as it is by the river from the old historical center and the ancient city, the district has always set itself apart from the rest of Rome. Once a working-class area, its inhabitants pride themselves on their attitude. Sass, pride, independence, toughness, and their own special accent all make *Trasteverini* a breed apart and lend a certain charm to a neighborhood that has retained its picturesque qualities. This aggressive attitude created an "us and them" opposition, with "us," *noantri*, being the *Trasteverini* and "them," *voiatri*, being all other Romans. The quarter's inhabitants celebrate what they see as superiority—reveling in being outsiders—during the *Festa de' Noantri*, a street fair held during the last two weeks of July.

Full of cafés, restaurants, bars, artisans, shops, boutiques, art galleries, and street vendors, it has for many years been a draw for bohemians—intellectuals, artists, filmmakers, and students. Its villagelike character, outsider pride, and hip lifestyle combine to give a slightly gritty edge to an area that, despite gentrification, has retained its authenticity. It is, after all, what the *Trasteverini* believe to be the home of true Romans.

PLACES TO SEE
Landmarks:

The atmospheric 15th-century footbridge **Ponte Sisto**  **(1)** *(at Lungotevere D. Farnesina)* is one of the most beautiful connecting links between Trastevere and the "other" Rome. It was built by Pope Sixtus IV della Rovere, who invested heavily in restoring churches and monuments and commissioning remarkable works of art and buildings, such as the Sistine Chapel and the Hospital of Santo Spirito.

As you step off the pedestrian bridge, you come upon **Piazza Trilussa** with its splendid fountain. The piazza honors the poet Carlo Alberto Salustri, a.k.a. Trilussa, a satiric 19th- and 20th-century poet who wrote in dialect and celebrated the spirit of Rome's everyman. Via Santa Dorotea, on the other side of the square, will bring you to the **Porta Settimiana (2)** *(see page 175)*, just inside of which is **Casa della Fornarina (3)** *(Via di Santa Dorotea 20; closed to the public)*, believed to have been the home of Margherita Luti, a baker's daughter *(fornarina)* and mistress of one of the early 16th century's great masters, Raphael.

The **Museo di Roma in Trastevere (4)** *(see page 167)*, an ethnographic museum of Roman folklore, was once a Carmelite convent attached to the church of Sant' Egidio. The highlight of the area, however, is **Santa Maria in Trastevere (5)** *(P.za Santa Maria in Trastevere, 06-581.48.02; hours: daily 7:30AM–8/9PM, may close 12:30PM–3:30PM)*, perhaps the first official Christian church in Rome. It was built in the 3rd century by Pope Callixtus I, well before Emperor Constantine legalized Christianity and ended the persecution of followers of the then-minor religion. The church was rebuilt in the 12th century by Pope Innocent II and still maintains its medieval characteristics.

Before Christianity was legal-ized, the followers of Christ worshipped in private houses, called *tituli*, built expressly for this purpose. Early 12th-century **San Crisogono (6)** *(P.za Sonnino 44, 06-581.82.25; hours: M–Sa 7AM–11AM, 4PM–7PM, Su 8AM–1PM, 4PM–7PM)* was built on top of a 5th-century church with 8th-century alterations, which was itself built on one of the oldest *tituli*. Excavations beneath this amazing building can be viewed. The church itself is full of recycled columns, marbles, and mosaics. More excavations—these dating from the 1st century AD—are of the barracks of the ancient Roman fire brigade, the **Caserma dei Vigili della VII Coorte (7)** *(Via della VII Coorte, 06-67.10.38.19; open by appt)*. You can see the courtyard where the firemen rested their weary feet. To rest your own weary feet, make your way over to **Piazza in Piscinula (8)**, beautiful despite all the parked cars.

The southeast sector of Trastevere is dominated by **Santa Cecilia in Trastevere (9)** (*P.za di Santa Cecilia, 06-589.92.89; hours: daily 9:30AM–12:30PM, 4PM–6:30PM*). On its grounds stood the home of Cecilia and her husband Valerianus, a patrician whom she converted to Christianity. The Romans attempted to behead her in AD 230, but it took her three days to die. During this time, she sang hymns, thus becoming the patron saint of music. According to legend, the saint's tomb was opened in 1599 and her body was found uncorrupted. Sculptor Stefano Maderno was commissioned to create a likeness of the martyr as she was found. The other masterpiece, or fragments of it, that is located within the church is the 13th-century fresco by Pietro Cavallini, *The Last Judgment*.

Near the Ripa Grande, the port area of Trastevere, was a hospice where St. Francis of Assisi stayed during his 1219 visit to Rome. In the 13th century, **San Francesco a Ripa (10)** (*P.za San Francesco d'Assisi 88, 06-581.90.20; hours: daily 7AM–12PM, 4PM–7PM*) was built on the site and rebuilt in the 17th century. The cell of St. Francis contains his crucifix and stone pillow as well as his portrait. One of the main highlights of this site is the Bernini sculpture *The Ecstasy of Beata Ludovica Albertoni*, a stunningly sexual rendition of the Franciscan nun's agony and ecstasy.

If Ludovica leaves you breathless, in need of fresh air and serenity, the **Chiostro dei Genovesi (11)** *(Via Anicia 12, bell marked "Sposito," no phone; hours: Apr–Sept Tu, F 3PM–6PM, Oct–Mar Tu, F 2PM–4PM)* is a fantastic cloister filled with flowers, the first palm tree planted in Rome (1588), and a charming well. You enter the cloister from a wooden door to the right of Santa Maria dell'Orto (the church with the obelisks). Otherwise, head for the park of **Villa Sciarra (12)** *(Via Calandrelli 35; Bus: 44, 75; hours: daily 9AM–sunset)* on the outskirts of Trastevere. Palm trees, manicured

lawns, and rose gardens as well as wild grasses helped in harboring Jews hiding from the Nazis during World War II.

Arts & Entertainment:

Rome's folklore depository, the **Museo di Roma in Trastevere (4)** *(P.za Sant'Egidio 1B, 06-581.65.63, www.museodiromaintrastevere.it; hours: Tu–Su 10AM–8PM)*, examines the daily life of common people in 18th- and 19th-century Rome. Its more interesting exhibits include wax replicas of places and people in Trastevere. The multilevel bookstore **Bibli (14)** *(Via dei Fienaroli 28, Cultural Center 06-581.45.34, Bookstore 06-588.40.97, www.bibli.it; hours: M 5:30PM–12AM, Tu–Su 11AM–12AM)* hosts readings, films, live music, and talks with film directors and writers. It also has a café and Internet access.

There are other noteworthy artistic venues in Trastevere. Don't miss **Big Mama (15)** *(Vicolo San Francesco a Ripa 18, 06-581.25.51, book ahead, www.bigmama.it; hours: daily 9PM–1:30AM, shows at 10:30PM)* if you love blues and R&B. Well-known acts, both Italian and international, play there. The live music (jazz, folk, rock) at **Lettere Caffè (16)** *(Via San Francesco a Ripa 100-101, 06-97.27.09.91, www.letterecaffe.org; call for hours)* is secondary to its literary readings, poetry slams, and book presentations. For theater and dance performances, catch a show at **Teatro Vascello (17)** *(Via Giacinto Carini 78, 06-588.10.21, www.teatrovascello.it; box office hours: Tu–Sa 4PM–9PM, Su 3PM–6PM)*, where productions might incorporate video and digital arts into theatrical works.

Independent films and art cinema are the focus of **Nuovo Sacher (18)** *(Largo Aschianghi 1, 06-581.81.16, www.sacherfilm.eu; call for showtimes)*, a movie theater owned by Italian director Nanni Moretti. Here you can catch films not picked up by mainstream distributors. The outdoor cinema is especially pleasant in summer; there's also a bar and bookshop. Another cinema, the three-screen multiplex **Pasquino (19)** *(P.za Sant'Egidio 10, 06-581.52.08; call for showtimes)*, shows films in their original language, mostly mainstream American and English movies.

PLACES TO EAT & DRINK
Where to Eat:

Traditional Roman cuisine doesn't come much better than at **Checco er Carettiere (20)** *(€€-€€€) (Via Benedetta 10, 06-580.09.85, www.checcoercarettiere.it; call for hours)*; pasta *all'amatriciana* is a typi-cal Roman dish. For a great ice cream place, try **Doppia Coppia (21) (€)** *(Via della Scala 51, 06-581.31.74; hours: Apr–Oct M–F 1PM–12AM, Sa–Su 1PM–1AM, Feb, Mar, Nov M–F 1PM–8PM, Sa–Su 1PM–10PM, closed Dec–Jan)*; the Sicilian owners concoct exotic flavors—cinnamon, *amarena*, *cassata*, or  coconut—and churn them into the most velvety cream.

Da Vittorio (22) (€) *(Via di San Cosimato 14A, 06-580.03.53; hours: M–Sa 7:30PM–12AM)*, on the other hand, is a wonderful neighborhood pizzeria, down to the checked tablecloths and straw-covered wine bottles. The pizzas make the establishment's soccer obsession clear: *Pizza Maradona* is named after the famous Argentinian soccer player while *Pizza Mondiale* gives a nod to the World Soccer Championship. When it comes to fish, Alberto Ciarla is a legend. From a famous family of restaurateurs and wine producers from the Castelli region near Rome, this aficionado of the sea's delicacies has one of the finest seafood restaurants in Rome. **Alberto Ciarla (23) (€€€)** *(P.za di San Cosimato 40, call after 5:30PM 06-*

581.60.68, www.albertociarla.com; hours: M–Sa 8:30PM–12AM) is a gourmet's mecca, with must-try fresh fish and shellfish dishes. Near the Porta Portese and its famous flea market *(see page 173)*, **Antico Tevere (60)** *(€€) (Via Portuense 45, 06-581.60.54; hours: M–Sa 1PM–3:30PM, 8:30PM–11:30PM)* serves Mediterranean-style seafood on a delightful terrace facing the Tiber. Try the *orecchiette alle vongole e zucchini*, octopus *bella vista*, or their fresh *strozzapreti* pasta.

Bars & Nightlife:

A popular beer hall, **La Scala (24)** *(P.za della Scala 58-61, 06-580.37.63, www.ristorantelascala.it; hours: daily 12PM–12:30AM)* is always crowded, a testament to its appeal. Get down and dirty with the rock 'n' roll and cheap drinks at **Big Hilda Café (25)** *(Vicolo dei Cinque  33-4, 06-580.33.03; hours: M–Sa 6:30PM–2AM, Su 12PM–2AM)*. Rub elbows with English ex-pats at **Mr. Brown (26)** *(Vicolo dei Cinque 29, 06-581. 29.13; call for hours)*, a sports pub with a musty British décor. Italians have a won-derful *aperitivo* tradition, and at **Friends Art Café (27)** *(P.za Trilussa 34, 06-581.61.11; hours: M–Sa 7:30AM–2AM, Su 6:30PM–2AM)* they do it very well: a free buffet assures the bar is crowded and enticing.

Let your hair down at **Stardust (28)** *(Vicolo dei Renzi 4, 06-58.32.08.75; hours: M–Sa 3:30PM–2AM, Su 12PM–2AM)*—an intimate, friendly bar where you're sure to meet the locals. It serves limited café food and brunch on Sundays. **Bar Trilussa (30)** *(Viale Trastevere 76, 06-580.91.31; call for hours)* is a typical Italian stand-up bar (or you can sit at a table outside). You'll find Roman workers, matriarchs, young people stopping in for a cappuccino and *cornetto* in the morning. It's the kind of friendly Italian café you dream about—the perfect place for an afternoon tea and pastry and a bit of local gossip.

On the outskirts of Trastevere near **Villa Sciarra (12)**, trendy **RipArte Caffè (61)** **(€-€€)** *(Via degli Orti di Trastevere 7, 06-586.18.16; call for hours)*, with its Italian-fusion and seafood specials, is a dinner and late-night hot spot. A bit farther south is another appealing restaurant, **Il Cortile (62)** **(€€)** *(Via Alberto Mario 26, 06-580.34.33; call for hours)*. A vegetable appetizer buffet, traditional Italian entrées, and yummy desserts are only part of the draw. Outdoor dining and the friendly owners also make the experience exceptional.

WHERE TO SHOP

Pandora della Malva (31) *(P.za San Giovanni della Malva 3, 06-581-34-06)* is a treasure trove of Venetian glass, from exquisite vases to beautiful necklaces; it also sells ceramics and offbeat, inexpensive jewelry. **Officina della Carta (32)** *(Via Benedetta 26b, 06-589.55.57)* is a true old-world stationery store. Handmade paper, cards, diaries, photo albums, and much more are made with a rare beauty and precision. Custom-made stationery, business cards, and invitations can be ordered. Art in

shoemaking characterizes the footwear at **Joseph Debach (33)** *(Vicolo dei Cinque 19, 06-556.27.56, www.josephdebach.com)*. Each pair is unusual, some with uncommon materials worked into the design—such as newspapers, wheels, or cobblestones. High-fashion designer fabrics in silk, linen, and cotton are the raw materials of the romantic ready-to-wear and custom-made women's clothing at **Scala Quattordici (34)** *(Via della Scala 14, 06-588.35.80)*.

The **Almost Corner Bookshop (35)** *(Via del Moro 45, 06-583.69.42)* is one of Rome's best English-language bookstores; the ivy-covered exterior is nearly as appealing as the cozy inside, which has a wide variety of books. Plaster architectural embellishments from **Eredi**

Baiocco (36) *(Via della Luce 3A, 06-58.33.10.68)* ornament some of Europe's most exclusive hotels. Bas-reliefs, statues, ceiling medallions, cornices, columns, pedestals, and many other types of decorating pieces can be shipped or wrapped up and carried home.

The famous **Porta Portese Flea Market (37)** *(Viale Trastevere, from Porta Portese to Trastevere Station, Sundays only, 7AM–2PM)*, the black market during World War II, may be the greatest flea market in Europe. Unique objects, modern clothes, the occasional great retro frock, odd items, and all sorts of bargains—and junk!—make it a shopper's paradise. Antiques, old laces and linens, costume jewelry, and bric-a-brac are concentrated in Via Ippolito Nievo.

WHERE TO STAY

A 17th-century palazzo turned into suites, **Residence in Trastevere (38)** (€€) *(Vicolo Moroni 35-36, 06-581.27.68, minimum one week)* is full of lovely details, such as open beams and a roof terrace with views of Gianicolo Hill. Once a 17th-century cloister, **Hotel Santa Maria (39)** (€€-€€€) *(Vicolo del Piede 2, 06-589.46.26, www.htlsantamaria.com)* is well protected from the noise of Trastevere's partylovers. The small but warmly furnished rooms look out over the courtyard with its orange trees, and the staff is very helpful. Attractive, with comfortable rooms, **La Cisterna (40)** (€) *(Via della Cisterna 8, 06-581.72.12, www.cisterna hotel.it)* is a small hotel in the heart of medieval Trastevere; the lovely courtyard has a fountain. **Trastevere (41)** (€) *(Via Luciano Manara 24A-25, 06-581.47.13 www.hoteltrastevere.net)* is a modest hotel with open-faced brick walls and small but pleasant rooms with a view of the market.

GIANICOLO

B: Botanic Gardens—23, 125, 280, 630, 780;
Palazzo Corsini—23, 60, 65, 125, 170, 280, 630, 780;
Bramante Tempietto—44, 75;
Garibaldi Monument—870

• SNAPSHOT •

To the north of the labyrinth of winding alleys of Trastevere is the marvelously bucolic Gianicolo Hill. The breathtaking panorama of the city vies with the beauty of the hill itself, especially its lovely Botanical Gardens. The main pathways of the hill lead to a piazza where the huge equestrian statue of Giuseppe Garibaldi stands as a monument to the man who fought for the unification of Italy and liberation from papal rule. The statue is on a terrace overlooking the city. Churches, monuments, Bramante's little temple, and the colossal fountain of the Paola Aqueduct are among the highlights of the Gianicolo. But most of all, when you've seen too many ancient ruins, when you have ceased to differentiate one ornate church from another, or when narrow, crowded streets begin to make you feel claustrophobic, the Gianicolo is the perfect remedy.

PLACES TO SEE
Landmarks:

From Trastevere, the most dramatic entrance into the Gianicolo is via the Renaissance **Porta Settimiana (2)**

(*between Via della Scala and Via della Lungara*). Via della Lungara passes beneath the gateway, a street built by Pope Sixtus V in the 16th century to connect Trastevere to the Vatican. Several notable villas were built along this road. In his sumptuous palace **Villa Farnesina (42)** (*Via della Lungara 230, 06-68.02.72.68; hours: M–Sa 9AM–1PM*), Agostino Chigi, the Vatican banker from Siena, entertained the high and the mighty of the 16th century. When he went bankrupt, his villa at the foot of the Gianicolo was bought by Cardinal Alessandro Farnese, who gave it its present name. Chigi was one of Raphael's important patrons, and the villa is full of stupendous, vividly colored frescoes by the master as well as others spectacularly painted by Baldassare Peruzzi.

The 17th-century Swedish Queen Christina was owner of **Palazzo Corsini (43)** (*Via della Lungara 10, 06-68.80.23.23, www.galleriaborghese.it; hours: Tu–Su 8:30AM–7:30PM*), known at the time as Palazzo Riario. Christina was famous for her grand library, her fabulous art collection of Old Masters, her commissioning music from Scarlatti and Corelli, and her many female and male lovers, the latter of whom were clergymen. The villa was later bought by the Corsini family and today houses the **Galleria Nazionale d'Arte Antica (43)** (*Palazzo Corsini*), part of the national art collection.

Behind Palazzo Corsini, at the foot of Gianicolo Hill, **Orto Botanico (44)** *(Largo Cristina di Svezia 24, 06-49.91.71.06/07)*, originally belonged to the Palazzo Corsini but is now the property of the University of Rome. A bamboo forest, palm trees, plants both indigenous to Italy and others from abroad, glorious flower beds, medicinal plants—all thrive in the lush, secluded splendor of the garden, where waterfalls, ponds, sculptures, and fountains add another dimension to the exotic flora.

Ascending Gianicolo Hill is a bit of a trek, but the incredible views of Rome make it worthwhile. Approaching from the south, there are a few notable landmarks along the way. **Porta San Pancrazio** *(Piazzale Aurelio)* is a lovely spot. Duck into the courtyard of **San Pietro in Montorio** to see Bramante's **Tempietto (45)** *(P.za San Pietro in Montorio, in the church's courtyard, 06-581.39.40; hours: Nov–Apr Tu–Su 9:30AM–12:30PM, 2PM–4PM, May–Oct Tu–Su 9:30AM–12:30PM, 4PM–6PM)*. It is, as  its name indicates, a little temple, round and domed, with Classical proportions and 16 Doric columns. It marks the place where some scholars believe St. Peter was crucified (the more accepted claim is that he was martyred where St. Peter's Basilica stands). Further up the hill, the monumental **Fontana dell'Acqua Paola (46)** *(Via Garibaldi)* is the visible manifestation of a 2nd-century aqueduct built by Emperor Trajan and restored by Pope Paul V, a Borghese—hence the change in name to Acqua Paola.

On a large, lively square, the enormous **Garibaldi Monument (47)** *(Piazzale Giuseppe Garibaldi)* commemorates Garibaldi and his Republican soldiers, who fought the French from the Gianicolo. North of the piazza is the **Anita Garibaldi Monument (48)** *(P.zzale A. Garibaldi)*, a dramatic equestrian statue of Garibaldi's Brazilian wife, who also fought valiantly against the French. Continuing north brings you past the **Manfredi Lighthouse** *(Viale Aldo Fabrizi)*, a gift of Italian Argentinians, to **Sant'Onofrio** *(P.za Sant'Onofrio 2)*, containing the tomb of Renaissance poet Torquato Tasso.

Arts & Entertainment:

The notable art collection at the state-owned **Palazzo Corsini/Galleria Nazionale d'Arte Antica (43)** *(see page 176)* also known as **Galleria Corsini**, includes works by Rubens, Van Dyck, Caravaggio, Fra Angelico, Guercino, Guido Reni, and Murillo, among others. **Teatro Ghione (49)** *(Via delle Fornaci 37, 06-637.22.94, www.teatroghione.it; box office hours: Tu–Sa 10:30AM–1PM, 4PM–8PM)*, beautiful and hip, is a desirable venue for well-known musicians and theater groups, both Italian and international. **Filmstudio (50)** *(Via degli Orti d'Alibert 1C, 06-45.43.97.75, www.filmstudioroma.com; call for showtimes)* was a focal point in the filmmaking scene of the 1960s. Now renovated, it continues to make its mark as one of the oldest art house cinemas in Rome. It's a one-of-a-kind place for independent films, video art, and experimental pieces from the '60s.

In the converted stables next door, London art dealer and patron Lorcan O'Neill opened **Galleria Lorcan O'Neill (51)** *(Via degli Orti d'Alibert 1e, 06-68.89.29.80, www.lorcanoneill.com; hours: M–F 12PM–8PM, Sa 2PM–8PM)* in response to the burgeoning art scene in Rome. The gallery has presented exhibitions of Italian and international artistic stars, such as Luigi Ontani, Tracey Emin, Kiki Smith, and Jeff Wall.

PLACES TO EAT & DRINK
Where to Eat:

Climb, crawl, or ride up Gianicolo Hill, but be sure to try **Antico Arco (53)** (€€–€€€) *(P.zale Aurelio 7, 06-581. 52.74, www.anticoarco.it; hours: daily 6PM–12AM)*, a hip, minimalist eatery. The chefs do magical things with fresh seasonal produce, transforming classical Roman dishes like spaghetti *cacio e pepe* (cheese and pepper) with a surprising sauce of zucchini flowers. After a vig-

orous walk on the hill, **Bar Gianicolo (54)** (€) *(P.zale Aurelio 5, 06-580.62.75; hours: Tu–Sa 6AM–1AM, Su 6AM–9PM)*, by the beautiful **Porta San Pancrazio** *(P.zale Aurelio)*, is a great pick-me-up. The *baretto* has exceptional snacks and lunch sandwiches at ridiculously low prices. Nearby, a local favorite, **Antica Pesa (55)** (€€) *(Via Garibaldi 18, 06-580.92.36, www.anticapesa.it; call for hours)*, offers traditional trattoria-style Roman food. **ATM Sushi Bar**

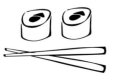

(56) (€€) *(Via della Penitenza 7, corner Via della Lungara, 06-68.30.70.53, www.atmsushibar.it; hours: Tu–Su dinner only, call for hours)* was the first sushi bar in Rome. Intimate and sleek, the interior is a striking combination of textures—iron, steel, wood, and leather—in blue and gray tones.

WHERE TO SHOP

Home decorations at **Laboratorio Ilaria Miani (57)** *(Via Orti d'Alibert 13A, 06-686.13.66)* include paintings, lamps, lampshades, and various interesting decorative pieces.

WHERE TO STAY

Atop Gianicolo Hill in an 18th-century villa, **Grand Hotel del Gianicolo (58)** (€€) *(Viale delle Mura Gianicolensi 107, 06-58.33.34.05, www.grandhotelgian icolo.it)* offers more than rooms done in marble and

appointed with Murano glass. The swimming pool, encircled by palm trees, is spectacular, and the extraordinary view from the roof garden makes you truly feel like you're at the top of the world. Exposed wood beams help embellish the simplicity of **Hotel la Rovere (59)** (€-€€) *(Vicolo di Sant'Onofrio 4-5, 06-68.80.67.39, www.hotellarovere.com)*, and some rooms have terraces. Single rooms are spare with few amenities, but doubles have A/C, heated towel racks, refrigerators, and bike rentals.

> If you're in search of more greenery, travel west to **Villa Doria Pamphili** *(Via di San Pancrazio, B: 31, 44, 75, 710, 870)*, one of the largest parks in Rome. It's a jogger's heaven.

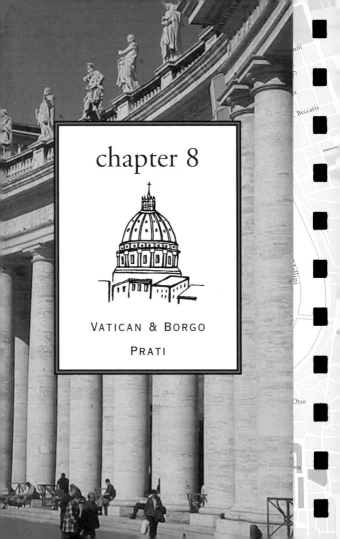

chapter 8

VATICAN & BORGO

PRATI

VATICAN & BORGO PRATI

Places to See:
1. St. Peter's Square
2. ST. PETER'S BASILICA ★
3. Vatican Gardens
4. Passetto
5. Hospital of Santo Spirito
6. Museum of Health Arts
7. Vatican Museums:
   RAPHAEL ROOMS ★
   SISTINE CHAPEL ★
20. Castel Sant'Angelo
21. Palazzo di Giustizia
22. Azzurro Scipioni

Places to Eat & Drink:
8. Caffè San Pietro
9. La Veranda dell'Hotel
   Columbus
10. Velando
11. Antica Latteria Giuliani
12. Nuvolari
23. Il Matriciano
24. Ottaviani
25. Dal Toscano
26. Il Simposio
27. Cremeria Ottaviani
29. Pellacchia
30. Alexanderplatz

31. The Place
32. BarBar

Where to Shop:
13. Savelli
14. Italia Garipoli
15. High-Tech d'Epoca
34. Gente
35. Vesti a stock
36. Mondadori
37. Maesano
38. Doctor Music
39. 40°
40. Costantini
41. Boccanera
42. Piazza dell'Unità
   Produce Market

Where to Stay:
16. Residenza Paolo VI
17. Hotel Bramante
18. Sant'Anna
19. Atlante Star
43. Hotel Colors
44. Hotel Alimandi Tunisi

★ *Top Picks*

VATICAN & BORGO

B: St. Peter's—23, 40, 62, 64;
Vatican Museums—23, 32, 34, 49, 81, 492

M: St. Peter's—A to Ottaviano-San Pietro;
Vatican Museums—A to Cipro-Musei Vaticani or
Ottaviano-San Pietro

• SNAPSHOT •

The Vatican lies on what was swampland in the 1st century BC. Emperor Caligula decided to build a circus—stadium—there for chariot races, a project completed by his nephew Nero when he became emperor in AD 54. Ten years later Nero began a campaign of persecution much larger than the one already being waged. Instead of chariot races, Nero's circus became the place where Christians were tarred and burned alive. It is believed that St. Peter, the apostle and first bishop of Rome (later called the pope or pontiff), was crucified in the circus and buried nearby. On his tomb in AD 326 Emperor Constantine built the first church of St. Peter, fulfilling the promise in the Gospel of St. Matthew: "You are Peter, and upon this rock I will build my church." Throughout the centuries, pilgrims continued to go to the tomb of St. Peter, the most sacred of Catholic shrines. The Borgo developed around this church, a "town" (or *burg*) to accommodate the religious tourists of the Dark Ages.

The Vatican is the smallest sovereign state in the world, with a population under 900 occupying 109 acres. Yet its political influence is felt the world over. The pope confers with world leaders and sways the political and social choices of millions of people around the globe.
The Vatican City is run as a state within a state, with its own police force (the Swiss Guard, with its plumes and exuberantly striped uniforms), a post office, Radio Vatican (which broadcasts to the world in 20 different languages), a daily newspaper *(L'Osservatore Romano)*, a publishing house, schools, an Internet domain (.va), shops, and the Vatican offices.

Pilgrims, tourists, and art lovers flock to the Vatican, irrespective of their religious leanings, to appreciate the beauty and majesty of its many masterpieces. The highlights are Piazza San Pietro, St. Peter's Basilica, the Vatican Museums, and the Vatican Gardens. The streets outside Piazza San Pietro—the Borgo—are full of restaurants, shops, and hotels.

DRESS CODE
The strictly enforced dress code in all parts of the Vatican City forbids shorts, short skirts, bare shoulders and knees, and exposed midriffs.

PLACES TO SEE
Landmarks:

Nowhere in the world is the extravagant wealth of the Catholic Church as evident as in the Vatican City. From the moment you enter **St. Peter's Square (1)**, you are overwhelmed by the grandeur and enormity of the place. An oval bound by two semicircular colonnades, the Piazza San Pietro was designed by Bernini in the mid-17th century. St. Peter's Square leads directly to ★**ST. PETER'S BASILICA (2)** *(P.za San Pietro, Vatican Switchboard 06-69.82, Vatican Tourism Office 06-69.88.16.62, www.saintpetersbasilica.org, www.vatican.va; hours: Basilica Apr–Sep 7AM–7PM, Oct–Mar 7AM–6PM; Treasury Museum Apr–Sep 9AM–6PM, Oct–Mar 9AM–5PM; Grottoes Apr–Sep 7AM–6PM, Oct–Mar 7AM–5PM; Cupola Apr–Sep 8AM–6PM, Oct–Mar 8AM–4:45PM;).* Of Rome's 650 or so churches, about 350 of them are in the city center; none is as opulent, magnificent, or awe-inspiring as St. Peter's. It is the heart of the Vatican State and the tomb of the founder of the Roman Catholic

Church. Construction on the present St. Peter's began in 1506 when Pope Julius II finally ordered the demolition of the original 4th-century church erected by Emperor Constantine, in a state of collapse after twelve centuries. For the next hundred years, a series of artists and architects worked on the new basilica,

TOP PICK!

each master changing the plans according to his vision. The main debate was whether the church should be shaped in the form of a Greek cross (four arms of equal length) or a Latin cross (a longer vertical segment with a shorter crossbar). Bramante, the original 1506 designer, envisioned a church similar to Santa Sophia, the Greek Orthodox cathedral in Constantinople; so his plan called for a Greek cross layout. When Raphael took over the project in 1514, he changed it to a Latin cross. Michelangelo, in 1547, switched it back to a Greek cross. He also created the plans for the present **dome of St. Peter's**, completed in 1590, 26 years after his death, and still the highest point in the city. Finally, in 1607, Pope Paul V made the decision: a Latin cross it would be, and Carlo Maderno was the architect to do it. The basilica was finally opened on November 18, 1626.

Five front doors lead into St. Peter's, the central ones taken from the original 4th-century church. The last door on the right is the **Porta Santa** (Holy Door), which is opened by the Pope only in Holy Years (every 25 years) and left open throughout that year. By the Holy Door, in a chapel to the right of the nave, is Michelangelo's famous marble masterpiece, the **Pietà**, which he sculpted when he was 25. Throughout the church and its chapels are works by master artists, including Bernini, Canova, and Algardi.

You can go up into Michelangelo's **dome** by climbing hundreds of stairs or taking the small elevator to the roof of the basilica, then climbing 320 slippery marble steps.

But once you've made it up there, what a breathtaking view! The Vatican Gardens, Rome, the world beyond—the panorama is magnificent.

> ### Survivor's Guide to the Vatican
>
> Keep a few things in mind when you set out for the Vatican. Noon is the least crowded time to go; Saturdays, Mondays, and religious holidays are especially crowded. Marble stairs, particularly in the dome, can be treacherous. Most of the areas—the Sistine Chapel excluded—are not air-conditioned, so it can get terribly hot. Some interesting details (like the ceiling of the Sistine Chapel) can't be seen up close. And be forewarned: the museum pieces are not well labeled at all. Therefore, take along the following essentials:
>
> • comfortable, nonslip shoes
> • bottled water
> • binoculars
> • guidebook specific to the museums

To the west of the basilica are the **Vatican Gardens (3)** *(Viale Vaticano)*, comprising 58 of the 109 acres of the Vatican. They can be visited only by taking a two-hour guided tour *(must be booked a week in advance via fax 06-69.88.46.76; pick up tickets 2–3 days before visit at Vatican info office, P.za San Pietro, left of basilica; for more* *info, Vatican Tourism Office, 06-69.88.16.62).* The grounds include formal Renaissance gardens with fountains and statues, tall palm trees, massive oaks, winding paths, and wildly colorful flowers.

Running along the north side of **Via della Conciliazione** is the **Passetto (4)** *(between Vatican and Castel Sant'Angelo)*, or Vatican Corridor, a covered aboveground escape route built during the Middle Ages for popes and their retinues to escape to the more fortified **Castel Sant'Angelo (20)** *(see page 195)*.

Nearby, the **Hospital of Santo Spirito (5)** *(Borgo Santo Spirito 2; hours: Chapel, daily 8:30AM–2PM)* has been taking care of abandoned babies and sick indigents since the early 13th century, when Pope Innocent III had a dream in which an angel took him to the Tiber to drag up the dead bodies of unwanted babies. The hospital's **Museum of Health Arts (6)** *(Lungotevere in Sassia 3, 06-689.30.51; hours: M, W, F 10AM–12PM, closed Aug)* has breathtaking frescoed walls, done in the Renaissance, as well as a room full of gruesome medical instruments.

Arts & Entertainment:

The patronage of popes over the centuries has resulted in an important collection of Classical and Renaissance art in the **Vatican Museums (7)** *(entrance to the museum complex in Viale del Vaticano, 06-69.88.33.33, www.vatican.va; hours: Mar–Oct M–F 8:45AM–4:45PM/last entrance at 3:20PM, Sa 8:45AM–1:45PM/last entrance 12:20PM; Nov–Feb M–Sa 8:45AM–1:45PM/last* *entrance 12:20PM).* Archaeological discoveries made in central Italy are also included in the collection, as are Egyptian, Etruscan, Greek, and Roman antiquities. The Etruscan Museum, Egyptian Museum, Pio-Christian Museum, Gregorian Profane Museum, and Vatican Library are among numerous others on the museum campus, all containing fascinating works. Several should not be missed.

TOP PICK!

The frescoes in the ★**RAPHAEL ROOMS**, Renaissance masterpieces, were created by Raphael and his students when Pope Julius II commissioned the master artist to decorate the four rooms of his private apartments. This work took over 16 years to finish and gave Raphael a reputation as illustrious as that of Michelangelo (who was working at the time on the Sistine Chapel, which he completed in four years, frescoing atop a special scaffolding). Raphael died before the work was finished, but his students fulfilled the master's vision.

TOP PICK!

The ★**SISTINE CHAPEL** is the main chapel of the Vatican Palace. Some of the most masterful artists of the 15th and 16th centuries created the frescoes on its walls, including Perugino, Ghirlandaio, Botticelli, and Signorelli. Michelangelo painted *The Last Judgment*, the fresco on the altar wall, as well as the chapel ceiling. The ceiling's central panels depict the Creation of the World, The Creation and Fall of Man, and The Story of Noah. The Classical Sibyls and Old and New Testament stories appear in the surrounding panels.

PLACES TO EAT & DRINK
Where to Eat:

Caffè San Pietro (8) (€) *(Via della Conciliazione 40-42, 06-687.14.72; call for hours)*, founded in 1775, is the second oldest Roman café operating today (after Caffè Greco in Piazza di Spagna, see page 62). As the only bar-restaurant in **Via della Conciliazione**,

it is full of customers, not a few of whom are clergy and officials from the Vatican. It's good for an Italian breakfast of cappuccino and *cornetti* (croissants) before a visit to the Vatican, or a lunch of Roman fare.

In the 15th-century Palazzo della Rovere near the Vatican, **La Veranda dell'Hotel Columbus (9) (€€€)** *(Borgo di Santo Spirito 73, off Via della Conciliazione, 06-687.29.73, www.hotelcolumbus.net; hours: daily 12:30PM–3:15PM, 7:30PM–11:15PM)* is delicious, romantic, and, with its original Pinturicchio frescoes, eye-popping. At **Velando (10) (€€)** *(Borgo Vittorio 26, 06-68.80.99.55, www.ristorantevelando.com; call for hours)* the owner is from Lombardy and the chef is from Apulia. In an Italian version of cultural diversity, North and South hit it off, and the food is fabulous. **Antica Latteria Giuliani (11) (€)** *(Borgo Pio 48, 06-68.80.39.55; call for hours)* is a good spot for breakfast or a quiet after-noon coffee.

Bars & Nightlife:

A typical Roman bar, **Nuvolari (12)** *(Via degli Ombrellari 10, 06-68.80.30.18; hours: M–Sa 6:30PM–2AM)* attracts locals as well as tourists for evening drinks.

WHERE TO SHOP

Via della Conciliazione, outside **St. Peter's (2)**, is full of shops selling religious articles and Vatican souvenirs. The place for religious mosaics is **Savelli (13)** *(Via Paolo VI 27-29, 06-68.30.70.17)*. Exquisite hand-embroidered lace and table and bed linens your grandmother would have loved are the specialty of **Italia Garipoli (14)** *(Borgo Vittorio 91, 06-68.80.21.96)*. They'll also mend lace. **High-Tech d'Epoca (15)** *(P.za Capponi 7, 06-687.21.47)*, run by an architect, specializes in antiques and office furniture from the early 1900s.

WHERE TO STAY

Once a monastery, **Residenza Paolo VI (16)** (€€) *(Via Paolo VI 29, 06-684.870/06-68.48.75.00, www.residenzapaolovi.com)* is a fine hotel overlooking the Vatican. The double rooms in what were monks' quarters are small but elegant, and the junior suites enjoy a beautiful view of the papal city. The former home of Renaissance architect Domenico Fontana, **Hotel Bramante (17)** (€€) *(Vicolo delle Palline 24, 06-68.80.64.26, www.hotelbramante.com)* has been beautifully restored, the rooms decorated with antique furnishings, and the sense of history underscored by the serene atmosphere.

The breakfast room frescoes and the courtyard fountain are some of the touches that give the small hotel **Sant'Anna (18)** (€€) *(Borgo Pio 133, 06-68.80.16.02, www.hotelsantanna.com)* its chic mark of distinction. The rooms are large, with small terraces adding allure to the top-floor spaces. The most exclusive of the hotels around the Vatican is the **Atlante Star (19)** (€€€-€€€€) *(Via Vitelleschi 34, 06-687.32.33, www.atlante hotels.com)*. Rooms are furnished with antiques, and the marble bathrooms have hot tubs. This sumptuous hotel has a huge roof garden with a view to die for.

PRATI

B: 23, 34, 40, 49, 70, 87, 280, 590, 926
M: A to Lepanto or Ottaviano-San Pietro

• SNAPSHOT •

Northeast of the Vatican and the Borgo lies Prati, a middle-class residential neighborhood of Rome. *Prati* means "fields." When Rome became the capital of unified Italy in 1871, the fields and meadows north of the Vatican were used to create housing for the staff of the new state. Prati became a bourgeois quarter of residences for people who worked in parliament and the ministries across the river. Elegant and peaceful, it has none of the vestiges of past eras—no ancient ruins, no narrow medieval streets, no Renaissance or Baroque garnishes. Rather, it reflects the contemporary life of middle-class Romans. It's also a shopping area, mostly along Via Cola di Rienzo and around Via Ottaviano. When the splendor of the Vatican's riches and the jostling of its crowds becomes unbearable, take a stroll through Prati, stop for lunch or an ice cream, and find some repose. Or go straight to Castel Sant'Angelo, Hadrian's fortress mausoleum that has been a prison as well as a papal refuge, to catch the beautiful Roman sunset.

PLACES TO SEE
Landmarks:

In the residential Prati district, the most spectacular landmark is **Castel Sant'Angelo (20)** *(Lungotevere Castello 50, entrance through gardens on right, 06-681.91.11, www.castelsantangelo.com; hours: Tu–Su 9AM–7PM/last entrance 6:30PM).* Built in the 2nd century as Emperor Hadrian's mausoleum, it underwent a series of changes in function: fortress, prison, papal residence. It formed part of Emperor Aurelian's wall encircling the city, and was a place of refuge for popes who were whisked there from the Vatican through the fortified **Passetto (4)** *(see page 189)* during various sackings of Rome. Today it is a museum chronicling the history of the fortress and serving as a space for temporary exhibitions. Hadrian had a spiral ramp built that leads to the upper terraces, where you  can see fabulous views of the city and its surroundings. It is from the top of **Castel Sant'Angelo (20)** that Tosca jumps to her death in the Tiber when she discovers, in the final scene of Puccini's opera, that the villain has murdered her lover, Mario.

The **Palazzo di Giustizia (21)** *(P.za Cavour, not open to the public),* the "Palace of Justice" law courts, built between 1889 and 1910 to right the injustices of papal rule, has not been immune to the corruption that has plagued Rome since Romulus killed Remus. Its façade is ornate and pompous, decorated with statues of Italian men of law and topped with a bronze chariot. Romans nicknamed it the *Palazzaccio*—the "big ugly palace."

Arts & Entertainment:

When you max out on antiquities, there's always the movies. **Azzurro Scipioni (22)** *(Via degli Scipioni 82, 06-39.73.71.61, www.azzurroscipioni.com; call for show-*

times) is a quirky movie theater with airplane seats. It shows films not seen elsewhere and classics, usually in the original language. All summer (June–September) in the gardens of **Castel Sant'Angelo (20)** a literary festival offers an opportunity to see Romans relaxing. Besides bookstalls and readings, there are also movies and outdoor eateries.

PLACES TO EAT & DRINK
Where to Eat:

Il Matriciano (23) (€€€€) *(Via dei Gracchi 55, 06-321.30.40/06-321.23.27; hours: daily 12:30PM–3PM, 8PM–11:30PM)* is a big, bright, friendly (albeit expensive) place with specialty meat dishes and a great antipasto plate with prosciutto, cheese, artichoke croquettes, and more. The pastas are delectable, and the *millefoglie*, a Napoleon layered with whipped cream, is divine. **Ottaviani (24)** (€) *(Via Paolo Emilio 9-11, 06-324.33.02; call*

for hours) offers you a wide range of choices for your pizza toppings.

For Tuscan specialties, go to **Dal Toscano (25)** (€€) *(Via Germanico 58, 06-39.72.57.17/06-39.72.33.73; call for hours)*, a popular eatery. An offshoot of **Costantini (40)**, one of Rome's best wine shops *(see page 198)*, **Il Simposio (26)** (€€€) *(P.za Cavour 16, 06-321.15.02/06-320. 35.75, www.pierocostantini.it; hours: M–Sa 12:30PM– 3PM, 7:30PM–11PM)* serves Roman dishes as delectable as its wines. Its Art Nouveau décor, walnut tables, and small but exceptional menu make this romantic little restaurant a sure thing.

There are a couple ice cream parlors in Prati that are worth a visit: **Cremeria Ottaviani (27)** (€) *(Via Leone IV 83-85, 06-37.51.47.74; closed W, call for hours)*; and **Pellacchia (29)** (€) *(Via Cola di Rienzo 103/111, 06-321.08.07/06-321.26.56; call for hours)* are sure to please the *gelato* lover.

Bars & Nightlife:
Alexanderplatz (30) *(Via Ostia 9, 06-39.74.21.71, www. alexanderplatz.it; hours: doors open 8PM, live concerts start 10)* is one of Italy's best jazz clubs, featuring the finest Italian and international jazz musicians. Another good jazz club is **The Place (31)** *(Via Alberico II 27-29, 06-68.30.71.37, www. theplace.it; call for hours)*, which showcases top-notch musicians. Stylish and hip, **BarBar (32)** *(Via*

Ovidio 17, 06-68.80.56.82, www.barbarroma.it; call for hours) is a lounge with good cocktails, subdued music, and a low-key clientele.

WHERE TO SHOP

Via Cola di Rienzo is a major shopping street in Prati. Clothing shops include ready-to-wear designer boutiques such as Max Mara, Calvin Klein, and Carla G., as well as stores like Diesel and Benetton. **Gente (34)** *(Via Cola di Rienzo 277, 06-321.15.16, www.genteroma.com)* promotes new designers and stocks well-known labels. For designer duds at discounts of 30 to 50%, check out **Vesti a stock (35)** *(Via Germanico 170a, 06-322.43.91)*. **Mondadori (36)** *(P.za Cola di Rienzo 81, 06-322.01.88)* is an Italian bookseller chain with a good stock of CDs

and DVDs. **Maesano (37)** *(P.za Cola di Rienzo 29, 06-321.56.74)* sells divine bed sheets and table linens. Jazz aficionados will love **Doctor Music (38)** *(Via dei Gracchi 41-43, 06-320.05.43)*; other musical genres are represented as well, in CDs and vinyl.

Vintage clothes and various *oggetti insoliti* capture the fancy at **40° (39)** *(Via Virgilio 1, at corner of Via Boezio, 06-68.13.46.12)*. **Costantini (40)** *(P.za Cavour 16, 06-321.32.10, www.pierocostantini.it)* is one of Rome's best wine shops. The cellar master helps you choose common or rare wines from all of Italy's 20 regions. Check out the shoes (Italian, of course!) at nearby

Boccanera (41) *(Via Vittoria Colonna 19, 06-320.44.56, www.boccanera.it)*. If you love browsing through lively farmers' markets, the **Piazza dell'Unità Produce Market (42)** has great stuff. Its stalls sell everything from fresh mozzarella, aromatic basil leaves, and fabulous smoked cold cuts to fish, meat, and Rome's favorite—zucchini flowers.

WHERE TO STAY

Bright primary colors enliven the hostel accommodations at **Hotel Colors (43)** (€) *(Via Boezio 31, 06-687.40.30, www.colorshotel.com)*. Some rooms share baths, and the dorm room sleeps five.

With its reproductions of classical statuary and its roof garden, the family-run **Hotel Alimandi Tunisi (44)** (€) *(Via Tunisi 1, 06-39.72.08.43, www.alimandi.it)* is pleasant and airy. It has a restaurant, gym, and plenty of spacious lounges. The rooms are large and amply furnished.

INDEX

NOTES

212

NOTES

NOTES

NOTES

NOTES

NOTES

NOTES

NOTES

PHOTO CREDITS